D1533288

TCP/IP Sockets in Java
Second Edition

The Morgan Kaufmann Practical Guides Series
Series Editor: Michael J. Donahoo

TCP/IP Sockets in Java: Practical Guide for Programmers, Second Edition
Kenneth L. Calvert and Michael J. Donahoo

SQL: Practical Guide for Developers
Michael J. Donahoo and Gregory Speegle

C# 2.0: Practical Guide for Programmers
Michel de Champlain and Brian Patrick

Multi-Tier Application Programming with PHP: Practical Guide for Architects and Programmers
David Wall

TCP/IP Sockets in C#: Practical Guide for Programmers
David Makofske, Michael J. Donahoo, and Kenneth L. Calvert

Java Cryptography Extensions: Practical Guide for Programmers
Jason Weiss

JSP: Practical Guide for Programmers
Robert Brunner

JSTL: Practical Guide for JSP Programmers
Sue Spielman

Java: Practical Guide for Programmers
Michael Sikora

Multicast Sockets: Practical Guide for Programmers
David Makofske and Kevin Almeroth

The Struts Framework: Practical Guide for Java Programmers
Sue Spielman

TCP/IP Sockets in C: Practical Guide for Programmers
Kenneth L. Calvert and Michael J. Donahoo

JDBC: Practical Guide for Java Programmers
Gregory Speegle

For further information on these books and for a list of forthcoming titles,
please visit our Web site at *http://www.mkp.com*.

TCP/IP Sockets in Java
Practical Guide for Programmers
Second Edition

Kenneth L. Calvert

University of Kentucky

Michael J. Donahoo

Baylor University

AMSTERDAM • BOSTON • HEIDELBERG • LONDON
NEW YORK • OXFORD • PARIS • SAN DIEGO
SAN FRANCISCO • SINGAPORE • SYDNEY • TOKYO

Morgan Kaufmann Publishers is an imprint of Elsevier

Publishing Director   Joanne Tracy
Publisher   Denise E. M. Penrose
Acquisitions Editor   Rick Adams
Publishing Services Manager   George Morrison
Senior Production Editor   Dawnmarie Simpson
Assistant Editor   Michele Cronin
Production Assistant   Lianne Hong
Cover Design   Alisa Andreola
Cover Images   istock
Composition   diacriTech
Technical Illustration   diacriTech
Copyeditor   JC Publishing
Proofreader   Janet Cocker
Indexer   Joan Green
Interior printer   Sheridan Books, Inc
Cover printer   Phoenix Color, Inc

Morgan Kaufmann Publishers is an imprint of Elsevier.
30 Corporate Drive, Suite 400, Burlington, MA 01803, USA

This book is printed on acid-free paper.

Library of Congress Cataloging-in-Publication Data
Calvert, Kenneth L.
    TCP/IP sockets in Java : practical guide for programmers / Kenneth L. Calvert, Michael J. Donahoo. – 2nd ed.
        p. cm.
    Includes bibliographical references and index.
    ISBN 978-0-12-374255-1 (pbk. : alk. paper) 1. Internet programming. 2. TCP/IP (Computer network protocol) 3. Java (Computer program language) I. Donahoo, Michael J. II. Title.
    QA76.625.C35 2008
    005.13'3–dc22

                                                                    2007039444

ISBN: 978-0-12-374255-1

For information on all Morgan Kaufmann publications,
visit our Web site at *www.mkp.com* or *www.books.elsevier.com*

Printed in the United States
08 09 10 11 12   5 4 3 2 1

To Tricia and Lisa

Contents

Preface

For years, college courses in computer networking were taught with little or no hands-on experience. For various reasons, including some good ones, instructors approached the principles of computer networking primarily through equations, analyses, and abstract descriptions of protocol stacks. Textbooks might have included code, but it would have been unconnected to anything students could get their hands on. We believe, however, that students learn better when they can see (and then build) concrete examples of the principles at work. And, fortunately, things have changed. The Internet has become a part of everyday life, and access to its services is readily available to most students (and their programs). Moreover, copious examples—good and bad—of nontrivial software are freely available.

We wrote this book for the same reason we wrote *TCP/IP Sockets in C*: We needed a resource to support learning networking through programming exercises in our courses. Our goal is to provide a sufficient introduction so that students can get their hands on real network services without too much hand-holding. After grasping the basics, students can then move on to more advanced assignments, which support learning about routing algorithms, multimedia protocols, medium access control, and so on. We have tried to make this book equivalent to our earlier book to enable instructors to allow students to choose the language they use and still ensure that all students will come away with the same skills and understanding. Of course, it is not clear that this goal is achievable, but in any case the scope, price, and presentation level of the book are intended to be similar.

Intended Audience

This book is intended for two audiences. The first, which motivated us to write it in the first place, consists of students in undergraduate or graduate courses in computer networks. The second consists of practitioners who know something about Java and want to learn about writing Java applications that use the Internet. We have tried to keep the book concise and focused, so it can be used by students as a supplementary text and by practitioners as a low-cost introduction to the subject. As a result, you should *not* expect to be an expert after reading this book! The goal is to take users far enough that they can start experimenting and learning on their own.

Readers are assumed to have access to a computer equipped with Java. This book is based on Version 1.6 of Java and the Java Virtual Machine (JVM); however, the code should work with earlier versions of Java, with the exception of a few new Java methods. Java is about portability, so the particular hardware and operating system (OS) on which you run should not matter.

Approach

Chapter 1 provides a general overview of networking concepts. It is not, by any means, a complete introduction, but rather is intended to allow readers to synchronize with the concepts and terminology used throughout the book. Chapter 2 introduces the mechanics of simple clients and servers; the code in this chapter can serve as a starting point for a variety of exercises. Chapter 3 covers the basics of message construction and parsing. The reader who digests the first three chapters should in principle be able to implement a client and server for a given (simple) application protocol. Chapters 4 and 5 then deal with increasingly sophisticated techniques for building scalable and robust clients and servers, with Chapter 5 focusing on the facilities introduced by the "New I/O" packages. Finally, in keeping with our goal of illustrating principles through programming, Chapter 6 discusses the relationship between the programming constructs and the underlying protocol implementations in somewhat more detail.

Our general approach introduces programming concepts through simple program examples accompanied by line-by-line commentary that describes the purpose of every part of the program. This lets you see the important objects and methods as they are used in context. As you look at the code, you should be able to understand the purpose of each and every line.

Our examples do not take advantage of all library facilities in Java. Some of these facilities, in particular serialization, effectively require that all communicating peers be implemented in Java. Also, to introduce examples as soon as possible, we wanted to avoid bringing in a thicket of methods and classes that have to be sorted out later. We have tried to keep it simple, especially in the early chapters.

What This Book Is Not

To keep the price of this book within a reasonable range for a supplementary text, we have had to limit its scope and maintain a tight focus on the goals outlined above. We omitted many topics and directions, so it is probably worth mentioning some of the things this book is not:

- It is not an introduction to the Java language. We focus specifically on TCP/IP socket programming. We expect that the reader is already acquainted with the language features and basic Java libraries—including those (like generics) introduced in later releases—and knows how to develop programs in Java.

- It is not a book on protocols. Reading this book will not make you an expert on IP, TCP, FTP, HTTP, or any other existing protocol (except maybe the echo protocol). Our focus is on the interface to the TCP/IP services provided by the socket abstraction. It will help if you start with some idea about the general workings of TCP and IP, but Chapter 1 may be an adequate substitute.

- It is not a guide to all of Java's rich collection of libraries that are designed to hide communication details (e.g., `HTTPConnection`) and make the programmer's life easier. Since we are teaching the fundamentals of how to do, not how to avoid doing, protocol development, we do not cover these parts of the API. We want readers to understand protocols in terms of what goes on the wire, so we mostly use simple byte streams and deal with character encodings explicitly. As a consequence, this text does not deal with `URL`, `URLConnection`, and so on. We believe that once you understand the principles, using these convenience classes will be straightforward.

- It is not a book on object-oriented design. Our focus is on the important principles of TCP/IP socket programming, and our examples are intended to illustrate them concisely. As far as possible, we try to adhere to object-oriented design principles; however, when doing so adds complexity that obfuscates the socket principles or bloats the code, we sacrifice design for clarity. This text does not cover design patterns for networking. (Though we would like to think that it provides some of the background necessary for understanding such patterns!)

- It is not a book on writing production-quality code. Again, although we strive for a minimum level of robustness, the primary goal of our code examples is education. In order to avoid obscuring the principles with large amounts of error-handling code, we have sacrificed some robustness for brevity and clarity.

- It is not a book on doing your own native sockets implementation in Java. We focus exclusively on TCP/IP sockets as provided by the standard Java distribution and do not cover the various socket implementation wrapper classes (e.g., `SocketImpl`).

- To avoid cluttering the examples with extraneous (nonsocket-related programming) code, we have made them command-line based. While the book's Web site, *books.elsevier.com/companions/9780123742551* contains a few examples of GUI-enhanced network applications, we do not include or explain them in this text.

- It is not a book on Java applets. Applets use the same Java networking API so the communication code should be very similar; however, there are severe security restrictions on the kinds of communication an applet can perform. We provide a very limited discussion of these restrictions and a single applet/application example on the Web site; however, a complete description of applet networking is beyond the scope of this text.

Acknowledgments

We would like to thank all the people who helped make this book a reality. Despite the book's brevity, many hours went into reviewing the original proposal and the draft, and the reviewers' input significantly shaped the final result.

Thanks to: Michel Barbeau, Chris Edmondson-Yurkanan, Ted Herman, Dave Hollinger, Jim Leone, Dan Schmidt, Erick Wagner, EDS; CSI4321 classes at Baylor University, and CS 471 classes at the University of Kentucky. Any errors that remain are, of course, our responsibility.

This book will not make you an expert—that takes years of experience. However, we hope it will be useful as a resource, even to those who already know quite a bit about using sockets in Java. Both of us enjoyed writing it and learned quite a bit along the way.

Feedback

We invite your suggestions for the improvement of any aspect of this book. If you find an error, please let us know. We will maintain an errata list at the book's Web site. You can send feedback via the book's Web page, *books.elsevier.com/companions/9780123742551*, or you can email us at the addresses below:

Kenneth L. Calvert—calvert@uky.edu

Michael J. Donahoo—Jeff_Donahoo@baylor.edu

chapter 1

Introduction

Today people use computers to make phone calls, to watch TV, to send instant messages to their friends, to play games with other people, and to buy almost anything you can think of—from songs to SUVs. The ability for programs to communicate over the Internet makes all this possible. It's hard to say how many individual computers are now reachable over the Internet, but we can safely say that it is growing rapidly; it won't be long before the number is in the billions. Moreover, new applications are being developed every day. With the push for ever increasing bandwidth and access, the impact of the Internet will continue to grow for the foreseeable future.

How *does* a program communicate with another program over a network? The goal of this book is to *start* you on the road to understanding the answer to that question, in the context of the Java programming language. The Java language was designed from the start for use over the Internet. It provides many useful abstractions for implementing programs that communicate via the application programming interface (API) known as *sockets*.

Before we delve into the details of sockets, however, it is worth taking a brief look at the big picture of networks and protocols to see where our code will fit in. Our goal here is *not* to teach you how networks and TCP/IP work—many fine texts are available for that purpose [4, 6, 12, 16, 17]—but rather to introduce some basic concepts and terminology.

1.1 Networks, Packets, and Protocols

A computer network consists of machines interconnected by communication channels. We call these machines *hosts* and *routers*. Hosts are computers that run applications such as your Web browser, your IM agent, or a file-sharing program. The application programs running on hosts are the real "users" of the network. Routers are machines whose job is to relay, or *forward*, information from one communication channel to another. They may run programs but typically do not run application programs. For our purposes, a *communication channel* is a means of conveying sequences of bytes from one host to another; it may be a wired (e.g., Ethernet), a wireless (e.g., WiFi), or other connection.

Routers are important simply because it is not practical to connect every host directly to every other host. Instead, a few hosts connect to a router, which connects to other routers, and so on to form the network. This arrangement lets each machine get by with a relatively small number of communication channels; most hosts need only one. Programs that exchange information over the network, however, do not interact directly with routers and generally remain blissfully unaware of their existence.

By *information* we mean sequences of bytes that are constructed and interpreted by programs. In the context of computer networks, these byte sequences are generally called *packets*. A packet contains control information that the network uses to do its job and sometimes also includes user data. An example is information identifying the packet's destination. Routers use such control information to figure out how to forward each packet.

A *protocol* is an agreement about the packets exchanged by communicating programs and what they mean. A protocol tells how packets are structured—for example, where the destination information is located in the packet and how big it is—as well as how the information is to be interpreted. A protocol is usually designed to solve a specific problem using given capabilities. For example, the *HyperText Transfer Protocol (HTTP)* solves the problem of transferring hypertext objects between servers, where they are stored or generated, and Web browsers that make them visible and useful to users. Instant messaging protocols solve the problem of enabling two or more users to exchange brief text messages.

Implementing a useful network requires solving a large number of different problems. To keep things manageable and modular, different protocols are designed to solve different sets of problems. TCP/IP is one such collection of solutions, sometimes called a *protocol suite*. It happens to be the suite of protocols used in the Internet, but it can be used in stand-alone private networks as well. Henceforth when we talk about the *network*, we mean any network that uses the TCP/IP protocol suite. The main protocols in the TCP/IP suite are the Internet Protocol (IP) [14], the Transmission Control Protocol (TCP) [15], and the User Datagram Protocol (UDP) [13].

It turns out to be useful to organize protocols into *layers*; TCP/IP and virtually all other protocol suites are organized this way. Figure 1.1 shows the relationships among the protocols, applications, and the sockets API (Application Programming Interface) in the hosts and routers, as well as the flow of data from one application (using TCP) to another. The boxes labeled TCP, UDP, and IP represent implementations of those protocols. Such implementations typically reside in the operating system of a host. Applications access the services provided by UDP and TCP through the sockets API. The arrow depicts the flow of data from the application, through the TCP and IP implementations, through the network, and back up through the IP and TCP implementations at the other end.

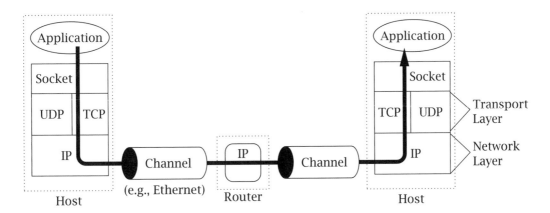

Figure 1.1: A TCP/IP network.

In TCP/IP, the bottom layer consists of the underlying communication channels—for example, Ethernet or dial-up modem connections. Those channels are used by the *network layer*, which deals with the problem of forwarding packets toward their destination (i.e., what routers do). The single network layer protocol in the TCP/IP suite is the Internet Protocol; it solves the problem of making the sequence of channels and routers between any two hosts look like a single host-to-host channel.

The Internet Protocol provides a *datagram* service: every packet is handled and delivered by the network independently, like letters or parcels sent via the postal system. To make this work, each IP packet has to contain the *address* of its destination, just as every package that you mail is addressed to somebody. (We'll say more about addresses shortly.) Although most delivery companies guarantee delivery of a package, IP is only a best-effort protocol: it attempts to deliver each packet, but it can (and occasionally does) lose, reorder, or duplicate packets in transit through the network.

The layer above IP is called the *transport layer*. It offers a choice between two protocols: TCP and UDP. Each builds on the service provided by IP, but they do so in different ways to provide different kinds of transport, which are used by *application protocols* with different needs. TCP and UDP have one function in common: addressing. Recall that IP delivers packets to hosts; clearly, a finer granularity of addressing is needed to get a packet to a particular application program, perhaps one of many using the network on the same host. Both TCP and UDP use addresses, called *port numbers*, to identify applications within hosts. TCP and UDP are called *end-to-end transport protocols* because they carry data all the way from one program to another (whereas IP only carries data from one host to another).

TCP is designed to detect and recover from the losses, duplications, and other errors that may occur in the host-to-host channel provided by IP. TCP provides a *reliable byte-stream* channel so that applications do not have to deal with these problems. It is a *connection-oriented* protocol: before using it to communicate, two programs must first establish a TCP connection, which involves completing an exchange of *handshake messages* between the TCP implementations on the two communicating computers. Using TCP is also similar in many ways to file input/output (I/O). In fact, a file that is written by one program and read by another is a reasonable model of communication over a TCP connection. UDP, on the other hand, does not attempt to recover from errors experienced by IP; it simply extends the IP best-effort datagram service so that it works between application programs instead of between hosts. Thus, applications that use UDP must be prepared to deal with losses, reordering, and so on.

1.2 About Addresses

When you mail a letter, you provide the address of the recipient in a form that the postal service can understand. Before you can talk to someone on the phone, you must supply a phone number to the telephone system. In a similar way, before a program can communicate with another program, it must tell the network something to identify the other program. In TCP/IP, it takes two pieces of information to identify a particular program: an *Internet address*, used by IP, and a *port number*, the additional address interpreted by the transport protocol (TCP or UDP).

Internet addresses are binary numbers. They come in two flavors, corresponding to the two versions of the Internet Protocol that have been standardized. The most common type is version 4 ("IPv4," [14]); the other is version 6 ("IPv6," [7]), which is just beginning to be deployed. IPv4 addresses are 32 bits long; because this is only enough to identify about 4 billion distinct destinations, they are not really big enough for today's Internet. (That may seem like a lot, but because of the way they are allocated, many are wasted. More than half of the total address space has already been allocated.) For that reason, IPv6 was introduced. IPv6 addresses are 128 bits long.

In writing down Internet addresses for human consumption (as opposed to using them inside programs), different conventions are used for the two versions of IP. IPv4 addresses are conventionally written as a group of four decimal numbers separated by periods (e.g., 10.1.2.3); this is called the *dotted-quad* notation. The four numbers in a dotted-quad string represent the contents of the four bytes of the Internet address—thus, each is a number between 0 and 255.

The sixteen bytes of an IPv6 address, on the other hand, are represented as groups of hexadecimal digits, separated by colons (e.g., 2000:fdb8:0000:0000:0001:00ab:853c:39a1). Each group of digits represents two bytes of the address; leading zeros may be omitted, so the fifth and sixth groups in the foregoing example might be rendered as just :1:ab:. Also, consecutive groups that contain only zeros may be omitted altogether (but this can only be done once in any address). So the example above could be written as 2000:fdb8::1:00ab:853c:39a1.

Technically, each Internet address refers to the connection between a host and an underlying communication channel—in other words, a *network interface*. A host may have several interfaces; it is not uncommon, for example, for a host to have connections to both wired

(Ethernet) and wireless (WiFi) networks. Because each such network connection belongs to a single host, an Internet address identifies a host as well as its connection to the network. However, the converse is not true, because a single host can have multiple interfaces, and each interface can have multiple addresses. (In fact, the same interface can have both IPv4 and IPv6 addresses.)

The *port number* in TCP or UDP is always interpreted relative to an Internet address. Returning to our earlier analogies, a port number corresponds to a room number at a given street address, say, that of a large building. The postal service uses the street address to get the letter to a mailbox; whoever empties the mailbox is then responsible for getting the letter to the proper room within the building. Or consider a company with an internal telephone system: to speak to an individual in the company, you first dial the company's main phone number to connect to the internal telephone system and then dial the extension of the particular telephone of the individual you wish to speak with. In these analogies, the Internet address is the street address or the company's main number, whereas the port corresponds to the room number or telephone extension. Port numbers are 16-bit unsigned binary numbers, so each one is in the range 1 to 65,535. (0 is reserved.)

In each version of IP, certain special-purpose addresses are defined. One of these that is worth knowing is the *loopback address*, which is always assigned to a special *loopback interface*, a virtual device that simply echoes transmitted packets right back to the sender. The loopback interface is very useful for testing because packets sent to that address are immediately returned back to the destination. Moreover, it is present on every host, and can be used even when a computer has no other interfaces (i.e., is not connected to the network). The loopback address for IPv4 is 127.0.0.1;[1] for IPv6 it is 0:0:0:0:0:0:0:1.

Another group of IPv4 addresses reserved for a special purpose includes those reserved for "private use." This group includes all IPv4 addresses that start with 10 or 192.168, as well as those whose first number is 172 and whose second number is between 16 and 31. (There is no corresponding class for IPv6.) These addresses were originally designated for use in private networks that are *not* part of the global Internet. Today they are often used in homes and small offices that are connected to the Internet through a *network address translation (NAT)* device. Such a device acts like a router that translates (rewrites) the addresses and ports in packets as it forwards them. More precisely, it maps (private address, port) pairs in packets on one of its interfaces to (public address, port) pairs on the other interface. This enables a small group of hosts (e.g., those on a home network) to effectively "share" a single IP address. The importance of these addresses is that *they cannot be reached from the global Internet*. If you are trying out the code in this book on a machine that has an address in the private-use class, and you are trying to communicate with another host that does *not* have one of these addresses, typically you will only succeed if the host with the private address initiates communication.

A related class contains the *link-local*, or "autoconfiguration" addresses. For IPv4, such addresses begin with 169.254. For IPv6, any address whose first 16-bit chunk starts with FE8

---

[1] Technically any IPv4 address beginning with 127 should loop back.

is a link-local address. Such addresses can *only* be used for communication between hosts connected to the same network; routers will not forward them.

Finally, another class consists of *multicast* addresses. Whereas regular IP (sometimes called "unicast") addresses refer to a single destination, multicast addresses potentially refer to an arbitrary number of destinations. Multicasting is an advanced subject that we cover briefly in Chapter 4. In IPv4, multicast addresses in dotted-quad format have a first number in the range 224 to 239. In IPv6, multicast addresses start with FF.

1.3 About Names

Most likely you are accustomed to referring to hosts by *name* (e.g., host.example.com). However, the Internet protocols deal with addresses (binary numbers), not names. You should understand that the use of names instead of addresses is a convenience feature that is independent of the basic service provided by TCP/IP—you can write and use TCP/IP applications without ever using a name. When you use a name to identify a communication endpoint, the system does some extra work to *resolve* the name into an address. This extra step is often worth it for a couple of reasons. First, names are obviously easier for humans to remember than dotted-quads (or, in the case of IPv6, strings of hexadecimal digits). Second, names provide a level of indirection, which insulates users from IP address changes. During the writing of the first edition of this book, the address of the Web server *www.mkp.com* changed. Because we always refer to that Web server by name, and because the change was quickly reflected in the service that maps names to addresses (about which we'll say more shortly)—*www.mkp.com* resolves to the current Internet address instead of 208.164.121.48—the change is transparent to programs that use the name to access the Web server.

The name-resolution service can access information from a wide variety of sources. Two of the primary sources are the *Domain Name System (DNS)* and local configuration databases. The DNS [10] is a distributed database that maps *domain names* such as *www.mkp.com* to Internet addresses and other information; the DNS protocol [11] allows hosts connected to the Internet to retrieve information from that database using TCP or UDP. Local configuration databases are generally OS-specific mechanisms for local name-to-Internet address mappings.

1.4 Clients and Servers

In our postal and telephone analogies, each communication is initiated by one party, who sends a letter or makes the telephone call, while the other party responds to the initiator's contact by sending a return letter or picking up the phone and talking. Internet communication is similar. The terms *client* and *server* refer to these roles: the client program initiates communication, while the server program waits passively for and then responds to clients that contact it.

Together, the client and server compose the *application*. The terms *client* and *server* are descriptive of the typical situation in which the server makes a particular capability—for example, a database service—available to any client that is able to communicate with it.

Whether a program is acting as a client or server determines the general form of its use of the sockets API to establish communication with its *peer*. (The client is the peer of the server and vice versa.) Beyond that, the client-server distinction is important because the client needs to know the server's address and port initially, but not vice versa. With the sockets API, the server can, if necessary, learn the client's address information when it receives the initial communication from the client. This is analogous to a telephone call—in order to be called, a person does not need to know the telephone number of the caller. As with a telephone call, once the connection is established, the distinction between server and client disappears.

How does a client find out a server's IP address and port number? Usually, the client knows the name of the server it wants—for example, from a *Universal Resource Locator (URL)* such as *http://www.mkp.com*—and uses the name-resolution service to learn the corresponding Internet address.

Finding a server's port number is a different story. In principle, servers can use any port, but the client must be able to learn what it is. In the Internet, there is a convention of assigning well-known port numbers to certain applications. The Internet Assigned Number Authority (IANA) oversees this assignment. For example, port number 21 has been assigned to the *File Transfer Protocol (FTP)*. When you run an FTP client application, it tries to contact the FTP server on that port by default. A list of all the assigned port numbers is maintained by the numbering authority of the Internet (see *http://www.iana.org/assignments/port-numbers*).

1.5 What Is a Socket?

A *socket* is an abstraction through which an application may send and receive data, in much the same way as an open file handle allows an application to read and write data to stable storage. A socket allows an application to plug in to the network and communicate with other applications that are plugged in to the same network. Information written to the socket by an application on one machine can be read by an application on a different machine and vice versa.

Different types of sockets correspond to different underlying protocol suites and different stacks of protocols within a suite. This book deals only with the TCP/IP protocol suite. The main types of sockets in TCP/IP today are *stream sockets* and *datagram sockets*. Stream sockets use TCP as the end-to-end protocol (with IP underneath) and thus provide a reliable byte-stream service. A TCP/IP stream socket represents one end of a TCP connection. Datagram sockets use UDP (again, with IP underneath) and thus provide a best-effort datagram service that applications can use to send individual messages up to about 65,500 bytes in length. Stream and datagram sockets are also supported by other protocol suites, but

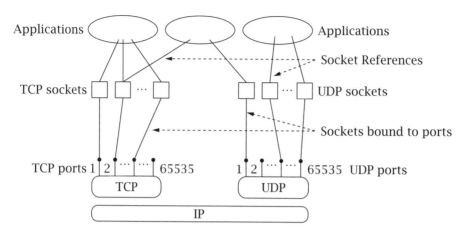

Figure 1.2: Sockets, protocols, and ports.

this book deals only with TCP stream sockets and UDP datagram sockets. A TCP/IP socket is uniquely identified by an Internet address, an end-to-end protocol (TCP or UDP), and a port number. As you proceed, you will encounter several ways for a socket to become bound to an address.

Figure 1.2 depicts the logical relationships among applications, socket abstractions, protocols, and port numbers within a single host. Note that a single socket abstraction can be referenced by multiple application programs. Each program that has a reference to a particular socket can communicate through that socket. Earlier we said that a port identifies an application on a host. Actually, a port identifies a socket on a host. From Figure 1.2, we see that multiple programs on a host can access the same socket. In practice, separate programs that access the same socket would usually belong to the same application (e.g., multiple copies of a Web server program), although in principle they could belong to different applications.

1.6 Exercises

1. Can you think of a real-life example of communication that does not fit the client-server model?

2. To how many different kinds of networks is your home connected? How many support two-way transport?

3. IP is a best-effort protocol, requiring that information be broken down into datagrams, which may be lost, duplicated, or reordered. TCP hides all of this, providing a reliable service that takes and delivers an unbroken stream of bytes. How might you go about providing TCP service on top of IP? Why would anybody use UDP when TCP is available?

chapter **2**

Basic Sockets

You are now ready to learn about writing your own socket applications. We begin by demonstrating how Java applications identify network hosts using the InetAddress and Socket-Address abstractions. Then we present examples of the use of Socket and ServerSocket, through an example client and server that use TCP. Then we do the same thing for the Datagram-Socket abstraction for clients and servers that use UDP. For each abstraction, we list the most significant methods, grouped according to usage, and briefly describe their behavior.[1]

2.1 Socket Addresses

Recall that a client must specify the IP address of the host running the server program when it initiates communication. The network infrastructure then uses this *destination address* to route the client's information to the proper machine. Addresses can be specified in Java using a string that contains either a numeric address—in the appropriate form for the version, e.g., 192.0.2.27 for IPv4 or fe20:12a0::0abc:1234 for IPv6—or a name (e.g., *server.example.com*). In the latter case the name must be *resolved* to a numerical address before it can be used for communication.

---

[1]**Note:** For each Java networking class described in this text, we include only the most important and commonly used methods, omitting those that are deprecated or beyond the use of our target audience. However, this is something of a moving target. For example, the number of methods provided by the Socket class grew from 23 to 42 between version 1.3 and version 1.6 of the language. The reader is encouraged and expected to refer to the API specification documentation from *http://java.sun.com* as the current and definitive source.

The InetAddress abstraction represents a network destination, encapsulating both names and numerical address information. The class has two subclasses, Inet4Address and Inet6Address, representing the two versions in use. Instances of InetAddress are immutable: once created, each one always refers to the same address. We'll demonstrate the use of InetAddress with an example program that first prints out all the addresses—IPv4 and IPv6, if any—associated with the local host, and then prints the names and addresses associated with each host specified on the command line.

To get the addresses of the local host, the program takes advantage of the Network Interface abstraction. Recall that IP addresses are actually assigned to the connection between a host and a network (and not to the host itself). The NetworkInterface class provides access to information about all of a host's interfaces. This is extremely useful, for example when a program needs to inform another program of its address.

InetAddressExample.java

```
0   import java.util.Enumeration;
1   import java.net.*;
2
3   public class InetAddressExample {
4
5     public static void main(String[] args) {
6
7       // Get the network interfaces and associated addresses for this host
8       try {
9         Enumeration<NetworkInterface> interfaceList = NetworkInterface.getNetworkInterfaces();
10        if (interfaceList == null) {
11          System.out.println("--No interfaces found--");
12        } else {
13          while (interfaceList.hasMoreElements()) {
14            NetworkInterface iface = interfaceList.nextElement();
15            System.out.println("Interface " + iface.getName() + ":");
16            Enumeration<InetAddress> addrList = iface.getInetAddresses();
17            if (!addrList.hasMoreElements()) {
18              System.out.println("\t(No addresses for this interface)");
19            }
20            while (addrList.hasMoreElements()) {
21              InetAddress address = addrList.nextElement();
22              System.out.print("\tAddress "
23                + ((address instanceof Inet4Address ? "(v4)"
24                    : (address instanceof Inet6Address ? "(v6)" : "(?)"))));
25              System.out.println(": " + address.getHostAddress());
26            }
27          }
28        }
```

```
29        } catch (SocketException se) {
30          System.out.println("Error getting network interfaces:" + se.getMessage());
31        }
32
33        // Get name(s)/address(es) of hosts given on command line
34        for (String host : args) {
35          try {
36            System.out.println(host + ":");
37            InetAddress[] addressList = InetAddress.getAllByName(host);
38            for (InetAddress address : addressList) {
39              System.out.println("\t" + address.getHostName() + "/" + address.getHostAddress());
40            }
41          } catch (UnknownHostException e) {
42            System.out.println("\tUnable to find address for " + host);
43          }
44        }
45      }
46  }
```

InetAddressExample.java

1. **Get a list of this host's network interfaces:** line 9
   The static method getNetworkInterfaces() returns a list containing an instance of
   NetworkInterface for each of the host's interfaces.

2. **Check for empty list:** lines 10-12
   The loopback interface is generally always included, even if the host has no other network
   connection, so this check will succeed only if the host has no networking subsystem
   at all.

3. **Get and print address(es) of each interface in the list:** lines 13-27

   ■ **Print the interface's name:** line 15
   The getName() method returns a local name for the interface. This is usually a combination of letters and numbers indicating the type and particular instance of the
   interface—for example, "lo0" or "eth0".

   ■ **Get the addresses associated with the interface:** line 16
   The getInetAddresses() method returns another Enumeration, this time containing
   instances of InetAddress—one per address associated with the interface. Depending
   on how the host is configured, the list may contain only IPv4, only IPv6, or a mixture
   of both types of address.

   ■ **Check for empty list:** lines 17-19

   ■ **Iterate through the list, printing each address:** lines 20-26
   We check each instance to determine which subtype it is. (At this time the only subtypes
   of InetAddress are those listed, but conceivably there might be others someday.) The

getHostAddress() method of InetAddress returns a String representing the numerical address in the format appropriate for its specific type: dotted-quad for v4, colon-separated hex for v6. See the synopsis "String representations" below for a description of the different address formats.

4. **Catch exception:** lines 29–31
   The call to getNetworkInterfaces() can throw a SocketException.

5. **Get names and addresses for each command-line argument:** lines 34–44
   - **Get list of addresses for the given name/address:** line 37
   - **Iterate through the list, printing each:** lines 38–40
     For each host in the list, we print the name returned by getHostName() followed by the numerical address returned by getHostAddress().

To use this application to find information about the local host, the publisher's Web server (*www.mkp.com*), a fake name (*blah.blah*), and an IP address, do the following:

```
% java InetAddressExample www.mkp.com blah.blah 129.35.69.7

Interface lo:
Address (v4): 127.0.0.1
Address (v6): 0:0:0:0:0:0:0:1
Address (v6): fe80:0:0:0:0:0:0:1%1
Interface eth0:
Address (v4): 192.168.159.1
Address (v6): fe80:0:0:0:250:56ff:fec0:8%4
www.mkp.com:
www.mkp.com/129.35.69.7
blah.blah:
Unable to find address for blah.blah
129.35.69.7:
129.35.69.7/129.35.69.7
```

You may notice that some v6 addresses have a suffix of the form %*d*, where *d* is a number. Such addresses have limited scope (typically they are link-local), and the suffix identifies the particular scope with which they are associated; this ensures that each listed address string is unique. Link-local IPv6 addresses begin with fe8.

You may also have noticed a delay when resolving blah.blah. Your resolver looks in several places before giving up on resolving a name. When the name service is not available for some reason—say, the program is running on a machine that is not connected to any network—attempting to identify a host by name may fail. Moreover, it may take a significant amount of time to do so, as the system tries various ways to resolve the name to an IP address. It is, therefore, good to know that you can always refer to a host using the IP address in dotted-quad notation. In any of the examples in this book, if a remote host is specified by name, the host running the example must be configured to convert names to addresses, or the example won't work. If you can ping a host using one of its names (e.g., run the command "ping *server.example.com*"), then the examples should work with names. If your ping test fails or the example hangs, try specifying the host by IP address, which avoids the name-to-address conversion altogether. (See also the isReachable() method of InetAddress, discussed below.)

InetAddress: Creating and accessing

```
static InetAddress[ ] getAllByName(String host)
static InetAddress getByName(String host)
static InetAddress getLocalHost()
byte[] getAddress()
```

The static factory methods return instances that can be passed to other Socket methods to specify a host. The input String to the factory methods can be either a domain name, such as "skeezix" or "*farm.example.com*", or a string representation of a numeric address. For numeric IPv6 addresses, the shorthand forms described in Chapter 1 may be used. A name may be associated with more than one numeric address; the getAllByName() method returns an instance for each address associated with a name.

The getAddress() method returns the binary form of the address as a byte array of appropriate length. If the instance is of Inet4Address, the array is four bytes in length; if of Inet6Address, it is 16 bytes. The first element of the returned array is the most significant byte of the address.

As we have seen, an InetAddress instance may be converted to a String representation in several ways.

InetAddress: String representations

```
String toString()
String getHostAddress()
String getHostName()
String getCanonicalHostName()
```

These methods return the name or numeric address of the host, or a combination thereof, as a properly formatted String. The toString() method overrides the Object method to return a string of the form "*hostname.example.com/192.0.2.127*" or "*never.example.net/2000::620:1a30:95b2*". The numeric representation of the address (only) is returned by getHostAddress(). For an IPv6 address, the string representation always includes the full eight groups (i.e., exactly seven colons ":") to prevent ambiguity when a port number is appended separated by another colon—a common idiom that we'll see later. Also, an IPv6 address that has limited scope, such as a link-local address will have a *scope identifier* appended. This is a local identifier added to prevent ambiguity (since the same link-local address can be used on different links), but is not part of the address transmitted in the packet.

The last two methods return the name of the host only, their behavior differing as follows: If this instance was originally created by giving a name, getHostName() will return that name with no resolution step; otherwise, getHostName() resolves the address to the name using the system-configured resolution mechanism. The getCanonicalName() method, on the other hand, always tries to resolve the address to obtain a *fully qualified domain name* (like "*ns1.internat.net*" or "*bam.example.com*"). Note that that address might differ from the one with which the instance was created, if different names map to the same address. Both methods return the numerical form of the address if resolution cannot be completed. Also, both check permission with the security manager before sending any messages.

The InetAddress class also supports checking for properties, such as membership in a class of "special purpose" addresses as discussed in Section 1.2, and reachability, i.e., the ability to exchange packets with the host.

┌─── **InetAddress : Testing properties** ─────────────────────────┐

```
boolean isAnyLocalAddress()
boolean isLinkLocalAddress()
boolean isLoopbackAddress()
boolean isMulticastAddress()
boolean isMCGlobal()
boolean isMCLinkLocal()
boolean isMCNodeLocal()
boolean isMCOrgLocal()
boolean isMCSiteLocal()
boolean isReachable(int timeout)
boolean isReachable(NetworkInterface netif, int ttl, int timeout)
```

These methods check whether an address is of a particular type. They all work for both IPv4 and IPv6 addresses. The first three methods above check whether the instance is one of, respectively, the "don't care" address, an address in the link-local class, or the loopback address (matches 127.*.*.* or ::1). The fourth method checks whether it is a multicast address (see Section 4.3.2), and the isMC...() methods check for various *scopes* of multicast address. (The scope determines, roughly, how far packets addressed to that destination can travel from their origin.)

The last two methods check whether it is actually possible to exchange packets with the host identified by this InetAddress. Note that, unlike the other methods, which involve simple syntactic checks, these methods cause the networking system to take action, namely sending packets. The system attempts to send a packet until the specified number of milliseconds passes. The latter form is more specific: it determines whetherthe destination can be contacted by sending packets out over the specified NetworkInterface, with the specified *time-to-live (TTL)* value. The TTL limits the distance a packet can travel through the network. Effectiveness of these last two methods may be limited by the security manager configuration.

The NetworkInterface class provides a large number of methods, many of which are beyond the scope of this book. We describe here the most useful ones for our purposes.

NetworkInterface: Creating, getting information

```
static Enumeration⟨NetworkInterface⟩ getNetworkInterfaces()
static NetworkInterface getByInetAddress(InetAddress addr)
static NetworkInterface getByName(String name)
Enumeration⟨InetAddress⟩ getInetAddresses()
String getName()
String getDisplayName()
```

The first method above is quite useful, making it easy to learn an IP address of the host a program is running on: you get the list of interfaces with getNetworkInterfaces(), and use the getInetAddresses() instance method to get all the addresses of each. *Caveat:* the list contains *all* the interfaces of the host, including the loopback virtual interface, which cannot send or receive messages to the rest of the network. Similarly, the list of addresses may contain link-local addresses that also are not globally reachable. Since the order is unspecified, you cannot simply take the first address of the first interface and assume it can be reached from the Internet; instead, use the property-checking methods of InetAddress (see above) to find one that is not loopback, not link-local, etc.

The getName() methods return the name of the *interface* (not the host). This generally consists of an alphabetic string followed by a numeric part, for example eth0. The loopback interface is named lo0 on many systems.

2.2 TCP Sockets

Java provides two classes for TCP: Socket and ServerSocket. An instance of Socket represents one end of a TCP connection. A *TCP connection* is an abstract two-way channel whose ends are each identified by an IP address and port number. Before being used for communication, a TCP connection must go through a setup phase, which starts with the client's TCP sending a connection request to the server's TCP. An instance of ServerSocket listens for TCP connection requests and creates a new Socket instance to handle each incoming connection. Thus, servers handle both ServerSocket and Socket instances, while clients use only Socket.

We begin by examining an example of a simple client.

2.2.1   TCP Client

The client initiates communication with a server that is passively waiting to be contacted. The typical TCP client goes through three steps:

1. Construct an instance of Socket: The constructor establishes a TCP connection to the specified remote host and port.

2. Communicate using the socket's I/O streams: A connected instance of Socket contains an InputStream and OutputStream that can be used just like any other Java I/O stream (see Section 2.2.3).

3. Close the connection using the close() method of Socket.

Our first TCP application, called TCPEchoClient.java, is a client that communicates with an *echo server* using TCP. An echo server simply repeats whatever it receives back to the client. The string to be echoed is provided as a command-line argument to our client. Some systems include an echo server for debugging and testing purposes. You may be able to use a program such as **telnet** to test if the standard echo server is running on your system (e.g., at command line "telnet server.example.com 7"); or you can go ahead and run the example server introduced in the next section.)

TCPEchoClient.java

```
0   import java.net.Socket;
1   import java.net.SocketException;
2   import java.io.IOException;
3   import java.io.InputStream;
4   import java.io.OutputStream;
5
6   public class TCPEchoClient {
7
8     public static void main(String[] args) throws IOException {
9
10      if ((args.length < 2) || (args.length > 3))  // Test for correct # of args
11        throw new IllegalArgumentException("Parameter(s): <Server> <Word> [<Port>]");
12
13      String server = args[0];       // Server name or IP address
14      // Convert argument String to bytes using the default character encoding
```

```
15      byte[] data = args[1] getBytes();
16
17      int servPort = (args.length == 3) ? Integer.parseInt(args[2]) : 7;
18
19      // Create socket that is connected to server on specified port
20      Socket socket = new Socket(server, servPort);
21      System.out.println("Connected to server...sending echo string");
22
23      InputStream in = socket.getInputStream();
24      OutputStream out = socket.getOutputStream();
25
26      out.write(data);  // Send the encoded string to the server
27
28      // Receive the same string back from the server
29      int totalBytesRcvd = 0;  // Total bytes received so far
30      int bytesRcvd;           // Bytes received in last read
31      while (totalBytesRcvd < data.length) {
32        if ((bytesRcvd = in.read(data, totalBytesRcvd,
33                        data.length - totalBytesRcvd)) == -1)
34          throw new SocketException("Connection closed prematurely");
35        totalBytesRcvd += bytesRcvd;
36      }  // data array is full
37
38      System.out.println("Received: " + new String(data));
39
40      socket.close();  // Close the socket and its streams
41    }
42  }
```

TCPEchoClient.java

1. **Application setup and parameter parsing:** lines 0–17
   - **Convert the echo string:** line 15
     TCP sockets send and receive sequences of bytes. The getBytes() method of String returns a byte array representation of the string. (See Section 3.1 for a discussion of character encodings.)
   - **Determine the port of the echo server:** line 17
     The default echo port is 7. If we specify a third parameter, Integer.parseInt() takes the string and returns the equivalent integer value.
2. **TCP socket creation:** line 20
   The Socket constructor creates a socket and connects it to the specified server, identified either by name or IP address, before returning. Note that the underlying TCP

deals only with IP addresses; if a name is given, the implementation resolves it to the corresponding address. If the connection attempt fails for any reason, the constructor throws an IOException.

3. **Get socket input and output streams:** lines 23-24
Associated with each connected Socket instance is an InputStream and an OutputStream. We send data over the socket by writing bytes to the OutputStream just as we would any other stream, and we receive by reading from the InputStream.

4. **Send the string to echo server:** line 26
The write() method of OutputStream transmits the given byte array over the connection to the server.

5. **Receive the reply from the echo server:** lines 29-36
Since we know the number of bytes to expect from the echo server, we can repeatedly receive bytes until we have received the same number of bytes we sent. This particular form of read() takes three parameters: 1) byte array to receive into, 2) byte offset into the array where the first byte received should be placed, and 3) the maximum number of bytes to be placed in the array. read() blocks until some data is available, reads up to the specified maximum number of bytes, and returns the number of bytes actually placed in the array (which may be less than the given maximum). The loop simply fills up *data* until we receive as many bytes as we sent. If the TCP connection is closed by the other end, read() returns −1. For the client, this indicates that the server prematurely closed the socket.

Why not just a single read? TCP does not preserve read() and write() message boundaries. That is, even though we sent the echo string with a single write(), the echo server may receive it in multiple chunks. Even if the echo string is handled in one chunk by the echo server, the reply may still be broken into pieces by TCP. One of the most common errors for beginners is the assumption that data sent by a single write() will always be received in a single read().

6. **Print echoed string:** line 38
To print the server's response, we must convert the byte array to a string using the default character encoding.

7. **Close socket:** line 40
When the client has finished receiving all of the echoed data, it closes the socket.

We can communicate with an echo server named *server.example.com* with IP address 192.0.2.1 in either of the following ways:

% **java TCPEchoClient server.example.com "Echo this!"**
Received: Echo this!
% **java TCPEchoClient 192.0.2.1 "Echo this!"**
Received: Echo this!

See TCPEchoClientGUI.java on the book's Web site for an implementation of the TCP echo client with a graphical interface.

Socket: Creation

```
Socket(InetAddress remoteAddr, int remotePort)
Socket(String remoteHost, int remotePort)
Socket(InetAddress remoteAddr, int remotePort, InetAddress localAddr, int localPort)
Socket(String remoteHost, int remotePort, InetAddress localAddr, int localPort)
Socket()
```

The first four constructors create a TCP socket and *connect* it to the specified remote address and port before returning. The first two do not specify the local address and port, so a default local address and some available port are chosen. Specifying the local address may be useful on a host with multiple interfaces. String arguments that specify destinations can be in the same formats that are accepted by the InetAddress creation methods. The last constructor creates an unconnected socket, which must be explicitly connected (via the connect() method, see below) before it can be used for communication.

Socket: Operations

```
void connect(SocketAddress destination)
void connect(SocketAddress destination, int timeout)
InputStream getInputStream()
OutputStream getOutputStream()
void close()
void shutdownInput()
void shutdownOutput()
```

The connect() methods cause a TCP connection to the specified endpoints to be opened. The abstract class SocketAddress represents a generic form of address for a socket; its subclass InetSocketAddress is specific to TCP/IP sockets (see description below). Communication with the remote system takes place via the associated I/O streams, which are obtained through the get...Stream() methods.

The close() method closes the socket and its associated I/O streams, preventing further operations on them. The shutDownInput() method closes the input side of a TCP stream. Any unread data is silently discarded, including data buffered by the socket, data in transit, and data arriving in the future. Any subsequent attempt to read from the socket will cause an exception to be thrown. The shutDownOutput() method has a similar effect on the output stream, but the implementation will attempt to ensure that any data already written to the socket's output stream is delivered to the other end. See Section 4.5 for further details.

Caveat: By default, Socket is implemented on top of a TCP connection; however, in Java, you can actually change the underlying implementation of Socket. This book is about TCP/IP, so for simplicity we assume that the underlying implementation for all of these networking classes is the default.

Socket: Getting/testing attributes

```
InetAddress getInetAddress()
int getPort()
InetAddress getLocalAddress()
int getLocalPort()
SocketAddress getRemoteSocketAddress()
SocketAddress getLocalSocketAddress()
```

These methods return the indicated attributes of the socket, and any method in this book that returns a SocketAddress actually returns an instance of InetSocketAddress. The InetSocketAddress encapsulates an InetAddress and a port number.

The Socket class actually has a large number of other associated attributes referred to as _socket options._ Because they are not necessary for writing basic applications, we postpone introduction of them until Section 4.4.

InetSocketAddress: Creating and accessing

```
InetSocketAddress(InetAddress addr, int port)
InetSocketAddress(int port)
InetSocketAddress(String hostname, int port)
static InetSocketAddress createUnresolved(String host, int port)
boolean isUnresolved()
InetAddress getAddress()
int getPort()
String getHostName()
String toString()
```

The InetSocketAddress class provides an immutable combination of host address and port. The port-only constructor uses the special "any" address, and is useful for servers. The constructor that takes a string hostname attempts to resolve the name to an IP address; the static createUnresolved() method allows an instance to be created without attempting this resolution step. The isUnresolved() method returns TRUE if the instance was created this way, or if the resolution attempt in the constructor failed. The get...() methods provide access to the indicated components, with getHostName() providing the name associated with the contained InetAddress. The toString() method overrides that of Object and returns a string consisting of the name associated with the contained address (if known), a '/' (slash), the address in numeric form, a ':' (colon), and the port number. If the InetSocketAddress is unresolved, only the String with which it was created precedes the colon.

2.2.2   TCP Server

We now turn our attention to constructing a server. The server's job is to set up a communication endpoint and passively wait for connections from clients. The typical TCP server goes through two steps:

1. Construct a ServerSocket instance, specifying the local port. This socket listens for incoming connections to the specified port.

2. Repeatedly:

   a. Call the accept() method of ServerSocket to get the next incoming client connection. Upon establishment of a new client connection, an instance of Socket for the new connection is created and returned by accept().

   b. Communicate with the client using the returned Socket's InputStream and OutputStream.

   c. When finished, close the new client socket connection using the close() method of Socket.

Our next example, TCPEchoServer.java, implements the echo service used by our client program. The server is very simple. It runs forever, repeatedly accepting a connection, receiving and echoing bytes until the connection is closed by the client, and then closing the client socket.

TCPEchoServer.java

```
0  import java.net.*;  // for Socket, ServerSocket, and InetAddress
1  import java.io.*;    // for IOException and Input/OutputStream
2
3  public class TCPEchoServer {
4
5    private static final int BUFSIZE = 32;   // Size of receive buffer
6
7    public static void main(String[] args) throws IOException {
```

```
8
9      if (args.length != 1)  // Test for correct # of args
10       throw new IllegalArgumentException("Parameter(s): <Port>");
11
12     int servPort = Integer.parseInt(args[0]);
13
14     // Create a server socket to accept client connection requests
15     ServerSocket servSock = new ServerSocket(servPort);
16
17     int recvMsgSize;   // Size of received message
18     byte[] receiveBuf = new byte[BUFSIZE];  // Receive buffer
19
20     while (true) { // Run forever, accepting and servicing connections
21       Socket clntSock = servSock.accept();     // Get client connection
22
23       SocketAddress clientAddress = clntSock.getRemoteSocketAddress();
24       System.out.println("Handling client at " + clientAddress);
25
26       InputStream in = clntSock.getInputStream();
27       OutputStream out = clntSock.getOutputStream();
28
29       // Receive until client closes connection, indicated by -1 return
30       while ((recvMsgSize = in.read(receiveBuf)) != -1) {
31         out.write(receiveBuf, 0, recvMsgSize);
32       }
33       clntSock.close();  // Close the socket.  We are done with this client!
34   }
35   /* NOT REACHED */
36   }
37 }
```

TCPEchoServer.java

1. **Application setup and parameter parsing:** lines 0–12
2. **Server socket creation:** line 15
   servSock listens for client connection requests on the port specified in the constructor.
3. **Loop forever, iteratively handling incoming connections:** lines 20–34
   - ■ **Accept an incoming connection:** line 21
     The sole purpose of a ServerSocket instance is to supply a new, connected Socket instance for each new incoming TCP connection. When the server is ready to handle a client, it calls accept(), which blocks until an incoming connection is made to the ServerSocket's port. (If a connection arrives between the time the server socket is constructed and the call to accept(), the new connection is queued, and in that case accept() returns immediately. See Section 6.4.1 for details of connection establishment.) The accept() method of ServerSocket returns an instance of Socket

that is already connected to the client's remote socket and ready for reading and writing.

■ **Report connected client:** lines 23–24
We can query the newly created Socket instance for the address and port of the connecting client. The getRemoteSocketAddress() method of Socket returns an instance of InetSocketAddress that contains the address and port of the client. The toString() method of InetSocketAddress prints the information in the form "/⟨address⟩:⟨port⟩". (The name part is empty because the instance was created from the address information only.)

■ **Get socket input and output streams:** lines 26–27
Bytes written to this socket's OutputStream will be read from the client's socket's InputStream, and bytes written to the client's OutputStream will be read from this socket's InputStream.

■ **Receive and repeat data until the client closes:** lines 30–32
The while loop repeatedly reads bytes (when available) from the input stream and immediately writes the same bytes back to the output stream until the client closes the connection. The read() method of InputStream fetches up to the maximum number of bytes the array can hold (in this case, BUFSIZE bytes) into the byte array (*receiveBuf*) and returns the number of bytes read. read() blocks until data is available and returns −1 if there is no more data available, indicating that the client closed its socket. In the echo protocol, the client closes the connection when it has received the number of bytes that it sent, so in the server we expect to eventually receive a −1 from read(). (Recall that in the client, receiving a −1 from read() indicates a protocol error, because it can only happen if the server prematurely closed the connection.)

As previously mentioned, read() does not have to fill the entire byte array to return. In fact, it can return after having read only a single byte. This write() method of OutputStream writes *recvMsgSize* bytes from *receiveBuf* to the socket. The second parameter indicates the offset into the byte array of the first byte to send. In this case, 0 indicates to take bytes starting from the front of *data*. If we had used the form of write() that takes only the buffer argument, *all* the bytes in the buffer array would have been transmitted, possibly including bytes that were not received from the client.

■ **Close client socket:** line 33
Closing the socket releases system resources associated with the connection, and is required for servers, because there is a system-specific limit on the number of open Socket instances a program can have.

┌─ **ServerSocket:** Creation ──┐

```
ServerSocket(int localPort)
ServerSocket(int localPort, int queueLimit)
ServerSocket(int localPort, int queueLimit, InetAddress localAddr)
ServerSocket()
```

A TCP endpoint must be associated with a specific port in order for clients to direct their connections to it. The first three constructors create a TCP endpoint that is associated with the specified local port and ready to *accept* incoming connections. Valid port numbers are in the range 0-65,535. (If the port specified is zero, an arbitrary unused port will be picked.) Optionally, the size of the connection queue and the local address can also be set. Note that the maximum queue size may not be a hard limit, and cannot be used to control client population. The local address, if specified, must be an address of one of this host's network interfaces. If the address is not specified, the socket will accept connections to any of the host's IP addresses. This may be useful for hosts with multiple interfaces where the server wants to accept connections on only one of its interfaces.

The fourth constructor creates a ServerSocket that is not associated with any local port; it must be *bound* to a port (see bind() below) before it can be used.

ServerSocket: Operation

```
void bind(int port)
void bind(int port, int queuelimit)
Socket accept()
void close()
```

The bind() methods associate this socket with a local port. A ServerSocket can only be associated with one port. If this instance is already associated with another port, or if the specified port is already in use, an IOException is thrown.

accept() returns a connected Socket instance for the next new incoming connection to the server socket. If no established connection is waiting, accept() blocks until one is established or a timeout occurs.

The close() method closes the socket. After invoking this method, incoming client connection requests for this socket are rejected.

ServerSocket: Getting attributes

```
InetAddress getInetAddress()
SocketAddress getLocalSocketAddress()
int getLocalPort()
```

These return the local address/port of the server socket. Note that, unlike a Socket, a ServerSocket has no associated I/O Streams. It does, however, have other attributes called options, which can be controlled via various methods, as described in Section 4.4.

2.2.3   Input and Output Streams

As illustrated by the examples above, the basic I/O paradigm for TCP sockets in Java is the *stream* abstraction. (The NIO facilities, added in Java 1.4, provide an alternative abstraction, which we will see in Chapter 5.) A stream is simply an ordered sequence of bytes. Java *input streams* support reading bytes, and *output streams* support writing bytes. In our TCP client and server, each Socket instance holds an InputStream and an OutputStream instance. When we write to the output stream of a Socket, the bytes can (eventually) be read from the input stream of the Socket at the other end of the connection.

OutputStream is the abstract superclass of all output streams in Java. Using an OutputStream, we can write bytes to, flush, and close the output stream.

OutputStream: Operation

```
abstract void write(int data)
void write(byte[ ] data)
void write(byte[ ] data, int offset, int length)
void flush()
void close()
```

The write() methods transfer to the output stream a single byte, an entire array of bytes, and the bytes in an array beginning at offset and continuing for length bytes, respectively. The single-byte method writes the low-order eight bits of the integer argument. These operations, if called on a stream associated with a TCP socket, may block if a lot of data has been sent, but the other end of the connection has not called read() on the associated input stream recently. This can have undesirable consequences if some care is not used (see Section 6.2).

The flush() method pushes any buffered data out to the output stream. The close() method terminates the stream, after which further calls to write() will throw an exception.

InputStream is the abstract superclass of all input streams. Using an InputStream, we can read bytes from and close the input stream.

InputStream: Operation

```
abstract int read()
int read(byte[ ] data)
int read(byte[ ] data, int offset, int length)
int available()
void close()
```

The first three methods get transfer data from the stream. The first form places a single byte in the low-order eight bits of the returned int. The second form transfers up to *data.length* bytes from the input stream into *data* and returns the number of bytes transferred. The third form does the same, but places data in the array beginning at offset, and transfers only up to length bytes. If no data is available, but the end-of-stream has not been detected, all the read() methods block until at least one byte can be read. All methods return −1 if called when no data is available and end-of-stream has been detected.

The available() method returns the number of bytes available for reading at the time it was called. close() shuts down the stream, causing further attempts to read to throw an IOException.

2.3   UDP Sockets

UDP provides an end-to-end service different from that of TCP. In fact, UDP performs only two functions: 1) it adds another layer of addressing (ports) to that of IP, and 2) it detects some forms of data corruption that may occur in transit and discards any corrupted messages. Because of this simplicity, UDP sockets have some different characteristics from the TCP sockets we saw earlier. For example, UDP sockets do not have to be connected before being used. Where TCP is analogous to telephone communication, UDP is analogous to communicating by mail: you do not have to "connect" before you send a package or letter, but you do have to specify the destination address for each one. Similarly, each message—called a *datagram*—carries its own address information and is independent of all others. In receiving, a UDP socket is like a mailbox into which letters or packages from many different sources can be placed. As soon as it is created, a UDP socket can be used to send/receive messages to/from any address and to/from many different addresses in succession.

Another difference between UDP sockets and TCP sockets is the way that they deal with message boundaries: *UDP sockets preserve them.* This makes receiving an application message simpler, in some ways, than it is with TCP sockets. (This is discussed further in Section 2.3.4.) A final difference is that the end-to-end transport service UDP provides is best-effort: there is no guarantee that a message sent via a UDP socket will arrive at its destination, and messages can be delivered in a different order than they were sent (just like letters sent through the mail). A program using UDP sockets must therefore be prepared to deal with loss and reordering. (We'll provide an example of this later.)

Given this additional burden, why would an application use UDP instead of TCP? One reason is efficiency: if the application exchanges only a small amount of data—say, a single request message from client to server and a single response message in the other direction—TCP's connection establishment phase at least doubles the number of messages (and the number of round-trip delays) required for the communication. Another reason is flexibility: when something other than a reliable byte-stream service is required, UDP provides a minimal-overhead platform on which to implement whatever is needed.

Java programmers use UDP sockets via the classes DatagramPacket and DatagramSocket. Both clients and servers use DatagramSockets to send and receive DatagramPackets.

2.3.1   DatagramPacket

Instead of sending and receiving streams of bytes as with TCP, UDP endpoints exchange self-contained messages, called datagrams, which are represented in Java as instances of DatagramPacket. To send, a Java program constructs a DatagramPacket instance containing the data to be sent and passes it as an argument to the send() method of a DatagramSocket. To receive, a Java program constructs a DatagramPacket instance with preallocated space (a byte[]), into which the contents of a received message can be copied (if/when one arrives), and then passes the instance to the receive() method of a DatagramSocket.

In addition to the data, each instance of DatagramPacket also contains address and port information, the semantics of which depend on whether the datagram is being sent or received. When a DatagramPacket is sent, the address and port identify the destination; for a received DatagramPacket, they identify the source of the received message. Thus, a server can receive into a DatagramPacket instance, modify its buffer contents, then send the same instance, and the modified message will go back to its origin. Internally, a DatagramPacket also has *length* and *offset* fields, which describe the location and number of bytes of message data inside the associated buffer. See the following reference and Section 2.3.4 for some pitfalls to avoid when using DatagramPackets.

DatagramPacket: Creation

```
DatagramPacket(byte[] data, int length)
DatagramPacket(byte[] data, int offset, int length)
DatagramPacket(byte[] data, int length, InetAddress remoteAddr, int remotePort)
DatagramPacket(byte[] data, int offset, int length, InetAddress remoteAddr, int remotePort)
DatagramPacket(byte[] data, int length, SocketAddress sockAddr)
DatagramPacket(byte[] data, int offset, int length, SocketAddress sockAddr)
```

These constructors create a datagram whose data portion is contained in the given byte array. The first two forms are typically used to construct DatagramPackets for receiving because the destination address is not specified (although it could be specified later with setAddress() and setPort(), or setSocketAddress()). The last four forms are typically used to construct DatagramPackets for sending.

Where offset is specified, the data portion of the datagram will be transferred to/from the byte array beginning at the specified position in the array. The length parameter specifies the number of bytes that will be transferred from the byte array when sending, or the maximum number to be transferred when receiving; it may be smaller, but not larger than data.length.

The destination address and port may be specified separately, or together in a SocketAddress.

DatagramPacket: Addressing

```
InetAddress getAddress()
void setAddress(InetAddress address)
int getPort()
void setPort(int port)
SocketAddress getSocketAddress()
void setSocketAddress(SocketAddress sockAddr)
```

In addition to constructors, these methods supply an alternative way to access and modify the address of a DatagramPacket. Note that in addition, the receive() method of DatagramSocket sets the address and port to the datagram sender's address and port.

DatagramPacket: Handling data

```
int getLength()
void setLength(int length)
int getOffset()
byte[ ] getData()
void setData(byte[ ] data)
void setData(byte[ ] buffer, int offset, int length)
```

The first two methods return/set the internal length of the data portion of the datagram. The internal datagram length can be set explicitly either by the constructor or by the setLength() method. Attempting to make it larger than the length of the associated buffer results in an IllegalArgumentException. The receive() method of DatagramSocket uses the internal length in two ways: on input, it specifies the maximum number of bytes of a received message that will be copied into the buffer and on return, it indicates the number of bytes actually placed in the buffer.

getOffset() returns the location in the buffer of the first byte of data to be sent/received. There is no setOffset() method; however, it can be set with setData().

The getData() method returns the byte array associated with the datagram. The returned object is a reference to the byte array that was most recently associated with this DatagramPacket, either by the constructor or by setData(). The length of the returned buffer may be greater than the internal datagram length, so the internal length and offset values should be used to determine the actual received data.

The setData() methods make the given byte array the data portion of the datagram. The first form makes the entire byte array the buffer; the second form makes bytes offset through offset + length − 1 the buffer. The second form always updates the internal offset and length.

2.3.2   UDP Client

A UDP client begins by sending a datagram to a server that is passively waiting to be contacted. The typical UDP client goes through three steps:

1. Construct an instance of DatagramSocket, optionally specifying the local address and port.

2. Communicate by sending and receiving instances of DatagramPacket using the send() and receive() methods of DatagramSocket.

3. When finished, deallocate the socket using the close() method of DatagramSocket.

Unlike a Socket, a DatagramSocket is not constructed with a specific destination address. This illustrates one of the major differences between TCP and UDP. A TCP socket is required to establish a connection with another TCP socket on a specific host and port before any data can be exchanged, and, thereafter, it *only* communicates with that socket until it is closed. A UDP socket, on the other hand, is not required to establish a connection before communication, and each datagram can be sent to or received from a different destination. (The connect() method of DatagramSocket does allow the specification of the remote address and port, but its use is optional.)

Our UDP echo client, UDPEchoClientTimeout.java, sends a datagram containing the string to be echoed and prints whatever it receives back from the server. A UDP echo server simply sends each datagram that it receives back to the client. Of course, a UDP client only communicates with a UDP server. Many systems include a UDP echo server for debugging and testing purposes.

One consequence of using UDP is that datagrams can be lost. In the case of our echo protocol, either the echo request from the client or the echo reply from the server may be lost in the network. Recall that our TCP echo client sends an echo string and then blocks on read() waiting for a reply. If we try the same strategy with our UDP echo client and the echo request datagram is lost, our client will block forever on receive(). To avoid this problem, our client uses the setSoTimeout() method of DatagramSocket to specify a maximum amount of time to block on receive(), so it can try again by resending the echo request datagram. Our echo client performs the following steps:

1. Send the echo string to the server.

2. Block on receive() for up to three seconds, starting over (up to five times) if the reply is not received before the timeout.

3. Terminate the client.

UDPEchoClientTimeout.java

```
0   import java.net.DatagramSocket;
1   import java.net.DatagramPacket;
2   import java.net.InetAddress;
3   import java.io.IOException;
4   import java.io.InterruptedIOException;
5
6   public class UDPEchoClientTimeout {
7
8     private static final int TIMEOUT = 3000;    // Resend timeout (milliseconds)
9     private static final int MAXTRIES = 5;      // Maximum retransmissions
10
11    public static void main(String[] args) throws IOException {
12
13      if ((args.length < 2) || (args.length > 3)) { // Test for correct # of args
14        throw new IllegalArgumentException("Parameter(s): <Server> <Word> [<Port>]");
15      }
16      InetAddress serverAddress = InetAddress.getByName(args[0]);  // Server address
17      // Convert the argument String to bytes using the default encoding
18      byte[] bytesToSend = args[1].getBytes();
19
20      int servPort = (args.length == 3) ? Integer.parseInt(args[2]) : 7;
21
22      DatagramSocket socket = new DatagramSocket();
23
24      socket.setSoTimeout(TIMEOUT);   // Maximum receive blocking time (milliseconds)
25
26      DatagramPacket sendPacket = new DatagramPacket(bytesToSend,  // Sending packet
27          bytesToSend.length, serverAddress, servPort);
28
29      DatagramPacket receivePacket =                              // Receiving packet
30          new DatagramPacket(new byte[bytesToSend.length], bytesToSend.length);
31
32      int tries = 0;      // Packets may be lost, so we have to keep trying
```

```
33    boolean receivedResponse = false;
34    do {
35      socket.send(sendPacket);          // Send the echo string
36      try {
37        socket.receive(receivePacket);  // Attempt echo reply reception
38
39        if (!receivePacket.getAddress().equals(serverAddress)) {// Check source
40          throw new IOException("Received packet from an unknown source");
41        }
42        receivedResponse = true;
43      } catch (InterruptedIOException e) {  // We did not get anything
44        tries += 1;
45        System.out.println("Timed out, " + (MAXTRIES - tries) + " more tries...");
46      }
47    } while ((!receivedResponse) && (tries < MAXTRIES));
48
49    if (receivedResponse) {
50      System.out.println("Received: " + new String(receivePacket.getData()));
51    } else {
52      System.out.println("No response -- giving up.");
53    }
54    socket.close();
55  }
56 }
```

UDPEchoClientTimeout.java

1. **Application setup and parameter processing:** lines 0–20

2. **UDP socket creation:** line 22
   This instance of DatagramSocket can send datagrams to any UDP socket. We do not specify a local address or port so some local address and available port will be selected. We could explicitly set them with the setLocalAddress() and setLocalPort() methods or in the constructor, if desired.

3. **Set the socket timeout:** line 24
   The timeout for a datagram socket controls the maximum amount of time (milliseconds) a call to receive() will block. Here we set the timeout to three seconds. Note that timeouts are not precise: the call may block for more than the specified time (but not less).

4. **Create datagram to send:** lines 26–27
   To create a datagram for sending, we need to specify three things: data, destination address, and destination port. For the destination address, we may identify the echo server either by name or IP address. If we specify a name, it is converted to the actual IP address in the constructor.

5. **Create datagram to receive:** lines 29–30
   To create a datagram for receiving, we only need to specify a byte array to hold the datagram data. The address and port of the datagram source will be filled in by receive().

6. **Send the datagram:** lines 32–47
   Since datagrams may be lost, we must be prepared to retransmit the datagram. We loop sending and attempting a receive of the echo reply up to five times.

   ▪ **Send the datagram:** line 35
   send() transmits the datagram to the address and port specified in the datagram.

   ▪ **Handle datagram reception:** lines 36–46
   receive() blocks until it either receives a datagram or the timer expires. Timer expiration is indicated by an InterruptedIOException. If the timer expires, we increment the send attempt count (*tries*) and start over. After the maximum number of tries, the while loop exits without receiving a datagram. If receive() succeeds, we set the loop flag *receivedResponse* to TRUE , causing the loop to exit. Since packets may come from anywhere, we check the source address of the recieved datagram to verify that it matches the address of the specified echo server.

7. **Print reception results:** lines 49–53
   If we received a datagram, *receivedResponse* is true, and we can print the datagram data.

8. **Close the socket:** line 54

Before looking at the code for the server, let's take a look at the main methods of the DatagramSocket class.

DatagramSocket: Creation

```
DatagramSocket()
DatagramSocket(int localPort)
DatagramSocket(int localPort, InetAddress localAddr)
```

These constructors create a UDP socket. Either or both of the local port and address may be specified. If the local port is not specified, or is specified as 0, the socket is bound to any available local port. If the local address is not specified, the packet can receive datagrams addressed to any of the local addresses.

DatagramSocket: Connection and Closing

```
void connect(InetAddress remoteAddr, int remotePort)
void connect(SocketAddress remoteSockAddr)
```

```
void disconnect()
void close()
```

The connect() methods set the remote address and port of the socket. Once connected, the socket can only communicate with the specified address and port; attempting to send a datagram with a different address and port will throw an exception. The socket will only receive datagrams that originated from the specified port and address; datagrams arriving from any other port or address are ignored. *Caveat:* A socket connected to a multicast or broadcast address can only *send* datagrams because a datagram source address is always a unicast address (see Section 4.3). Note that connecting is strictly a local operation because (unlike TCP) there is no end-to-end packet exchange involved. disconnect() unsets the remote address and port, if any. The close() method indicates that the socket is no longer in use; further attempts to send or receive throw an exception.

DatagramSocket: Addressing

```
InetAddress getInetAddress()
int getPort()
SocketAddress getRemoteSocketAddress()
InetAddress getLocalAddress()
int getLocalPort()
SocketAddress getLocalSocketAddress()
```

The first method returns an InetAddress instance representing the address of the remote socket to which this socket is connected, or null if it is not connected. Similarly, getPort() returns the port number to which the socket is connected, or −1 if it is not connected. The third method returns both address and port conveniently encapsulated in an instance of SocketAddress, or null if unconnected.

The last three methods provide the same service for the *local* address and port. If the socket has not been bound to a local address, getLocalAddress() returns the wildcard ("any local address") address. getLocalPort() always returns a local port number; if the socket was not been bound before the call, the call causes the socket to be bound to any available local port. The getLocalSocketAddress() returns null if the socket is not bound.

DatagramSocket: Sending and receiving

```
void send(DatagramPacket packet)
void receive(DatagramPacket packet)
```

The send() method sends the DatagramPacket. If connected, the packet is sent to the address to which the socket is connected, unless the DatagramPacket specifies a different destination, in which case an exception is thrown. Otherwise, the packet is sent to the destination indicated by the DatagramPacket. This method does not block.

The receive() method blocks until a datagram is received, and then copies its data into the given DatagramPacket. If the socket is connected, the method blocks until a datagram is received from the remote socket to which it is connected.

DatagramSocket: Options

```
int getSoTimeout()
void setSoTimeout(int timeoutMillis)
```

These methods return and set, respectively, the maximum amount of time that a receive() call will block for this socket. If the timer expires before data is available, an InterruptedIOException is thrown. The timeout value is given in milliseconds.

Like Socket and ServerSocket, the DatagramSocket class has many other options. They are described more fully in Section 4.4.

2.3.3   UDP Server

Like a TCP server, a UDP server's job is to set up a communication endpoint and passively wait for clients to initiate communication; however, since UDP is connectionless, UDP communication is initiated by a datagram from the client, without going through a connection setup as in TCP. The typical UDP server goes through three steps:

1. Construct an instance of DatagramSocket, specifying the local port and, optionally, the local address. The server is now ready to receive datagrams from any client.

2. Receive an instance of DatagramPacket using the receive() method of DatagramSocket. When receive() returns, the datagram contains the client's address so we know where to send the reply.

3. Communicate by sending and receiving DatagramPackets using the send() and receive() methods of DatagramSocket.

Our next program example, UDPEchoServer.java, implements the UDP version of the echo server. The server is very simple: it loops forever, receiving datagrams and then sending the same datagrams back to the client. Actually, our server only receives and sends back the first 255 (*ECHOMAX*) characters of the datagram; any excess is silently discarded by the socket implementation (see Section 2.3.4).

UDPEchoServer.java

```
0  import java.io.IOException;
1  import java.net.DatagramPacket;
2  import java.net.DatagramSocket;
3
4  public class UDPEchoServer {
5
6    private static final int ECHOMAX = 255; // Maximum size of echo datagram
7
8    public static void main(String[] args) throws IOException {
9
10     if (args.length != 1) { // Test for correct argument list
11       throw new IllegalArgumentException("Parameter(s): <Port>");
12     }
13
14     int servPort = Integer.parseInt(args[0]);
15
16     DatagramSocket socket = new DatagramSocket(servPort);
17     DatagramPacket packet = new DatagramPacket(new byte[ECHOMAX], ECHOMAX);
18
19     while (true) { // Run forever, receiving and echoing datagrams
20       socket.receive(packet); // Receive packet from client
21       System.out.println("Handling client at " + packet.getAddress().getHostAddress()
22                                         + " on port " + packet.getPort());
23       socket.send(packet); // Send the same packet back to client
24       packet.setLength(ECHOMAX); // Reset length to avoid shrinking buffer
25     }
26     /* NOT REACHED */
27   }
28 }
```

UDPEchoServer.java

1. **Application setup and parameter parsing:** lines 0–14
   UDPEchoServer takes a single parameter, the local port of the echo server socket.

2. **Create and set up datagram socket:** line 16
   Unlike our UDP client, a UDP server must explicitly set its local port to a number known by the client; otherwise, the client will not know the destination port for its echo request datagram. When the server receives the echo datagram from the client, it can find out the client's address and port from the datagram.

3. **Create datagram:** line 17
   UDP messages are contained in datagrams. We construct an instance of DatagramPacket with a buffer of *ECHOMAX* 255 bytes. This datagram will be used both to receive the echo request and to send the echo reply.

4. **Iteratively handle incoming echo requests:** lines 19–25
   The UDP server uses a single socket for all communication, unlike the TCP server, which creates a new socket with every successful accept().

   ▪ **Receive echo request datagram, print source:** lines 20–22
   The receive() method of DatagramSocket blocks until a datagram is received from a client (unless a timeout is set). There is no connection, so each datagram may come from a different sender. The datagram itself contains the sender's (client's) source address and port.

   ▪ **Send echo reply:** line 23
   packet already contains the echo string and echo reply destination address and port, so the send() method of DatagramSocket can simply transmit the datagram previously received. Note that when we receive the datagram, we interpret the datagram address and port as the *source* address and port, and when we send a datagram, we interpret the datagram's address and port as the *destination* address and port.

   ▪ **Reset buffer size:** line 24
   The internal length of *packet* was set to the length of the message just processed, which may have been smaller than the original buffer size. If we do not reset the internal length before receiving again, the next message will be truncated if it is longer than the one just received.

2.3.4 Sending and Receiving with UDP Sockets

In this section we consider some of the differences between communicating with UDP sockets compared to TCP. A subtle but important difference is that UDP preserves message boundaries. Each call to receive() on a DatagramSocket returns data from at most one call to send(). Moreover, different calls to receive() will never return data from the same call to send().

When a call to write() on a TCP socket's output stream returns, all the caller knows is that the data has been copied into a buffer for transmission; the data may or may not have actually been transmitted yet. (This is covered in more detail in Chapter 6.) UDP, however, does not provide recovery from network errors and, therefore, does not buffer data for possible retransmission. This means that by the time a call to send() returns, the message has been passed to the underlying channel for transmission and is (or soon will be) on its way out the door.

Between the time a message arrives from the network and the time its data is returned via read() or receive(), the data is stored in a *first-in, first-out (FIFO)* queue of received data. With a connected TCP socket, all received-but-not-yet-delivered bytes are treated as one continuous sequence of bytes (see Chapter 6). For a UDP socket, however, the received data may have come from different senders. A UDP socket's received data is kept in a queue of messages, each with associated information identifying its source. A call to receive() will never return more than one message. However, if receive() is called with a DatagramPacket containing a buffer of size n, and the size of the first message in the receive queue exceeds n, only the first n bytes of the message are returned. The remaining bytes are quietly discarded, with no indication to the receiving program that information has been lost!

For this reason, a receiver should always supply a DatagramPacket that has enough space to hold the largest message allowed by the application protocol at the time it calls to receive(). This technique will guarantee that no data will be lost. The maximum amount of data that can be transmitted in a DatagramPacket is 65,507 bytes—the largest payload that can be carried in a UDP datagram. Thus it's always safe to use a packet that has an array of size 65,600 or so.

It is also important to remember here that each instance of DatagramPacket has an internal notion of message length that may be changed whenever a message is received into that instance (to reflect the number of bytes in the received message). Applications that call receive() more than once with the same instance of DatagramPacket should explicitly reset the internal length to the actual buffer length before each subsequent call to receive().

Another potential source of problems for beginners is the getData() method of DatagramPacket, which always returns the entire original buffer, ignoring the internal offset and length values. Receiving a message into the DatagramPacket only modifies those locations of the buffer into which message data was placed. For example, suppose *buf* is a byte array of size 20, which has been initialized so that each byte contains its index in the array:

0	1	2	3	4	5	6	7	8	9	10	11	12	13	14	15	16	17	18	19

Suppose also that *dg* is a DatagramPacket, and that we set *dg*'s buffer to be the middle 10 bytes of *buf*:

```
dg.setData(buf,5,10);
```

Now suppose that *dgsocket* is a DatagramSocket, and that somebody sends an 8-byte message containing

41	42	43	44	45	46	47	48

to *dgsocket*. The message is received into *dg*:

```
dgsocket.receive(dg);
```

Now, calling *dg*.getData() returns a reference to the original byte array *buf*, whose contents are now

0	1	2	3	4	41	42	43	44	45	46	47	48	13	14	15	16	17	18	19

Note that only bytes 5–12 of *buf* have been modified and that, in general, the application needs to use getOffset() and getData() to access just the received data. One possibility is to copy the received data into a separate byte array, like this:

```
byte[] destBuf = new byte[dg.getLength()];
System.arraycopy(dg.getData(), dg.getOffset(), destBuf, 0, destBuf.length);
```

As of Java 1.6, we can do it in one step using the convenience method Arrays.copyOfRange():

```
byte[] destBuf = Arrays.copyOfRange(dg.getData(),dg.getOffset(),
                    dg.getOffset()+dg.getLength());
```

We didn't have to do this copying in `UDPEchoServer.java` because the server did not read the data from the `DatagramPacket` at all.

2.4 Exercises

1. For `TCPEchoServer.java`, we explicitly specify the port to the socket in the constructor. We said that a socket must have a port for communication, yet we do not specify a port in `TCPEchoClient.java`. How is the echo client's socket assigned a port?

2. When you make a phone call, it is usually the callee that answers with "Hello." What changes to our client and server examples would be needed to implement this?

3. What happens if a TCP server never calls `accept()`? What happens if a TCP client sends data on a socket that has not yet been `accept()`ed at the server?

4. Servers are supposed to run for a long time without stopping—therefore, they must be designed to provide good service no matter what their clients do. Examine the server examples (`TCPEchoServer.java` and `UDPEchoServer.java`) and list anything you can think of that a client might do to cause it to give poor service to other clients. Suggest improvements to fix the problems that you find.

5. Modify `TCPEchoServer.java` to read and write only a single byte at a time, sleeping one second between each byte. Verify that `TCPEchoClient.java` requires multiple reads to successfully receive the entire echo string, even though it sent the echo string with one `write()`.

6. Modify `TCPEchoServer.java` to read and write a single byte and then close the socket. What happens when the `TCPEchoClient` sends a multibyte string to this server? What is happening? (Note that the response could vary by OS.)

7. Modify `UDPEchoServer.java` so that it only echoes every other datagram it receives. Verify that `UDPEchoClientTimeout.java` retransmits datagrams until it either receives a reply or exceeds the number of retries.

8. Modify `UDPEchoServer.java` so that *ECHOMAX* is much shorter (say, 5 bytes). Then use `UDPEchoClientTimeout.java` to send an echo string that is too long. What happens?

9. Verify experimentally the size of the largest message you can send and receive using a `DatagramPacket`.

10. While `UDPEchoServer.java` explicitly specifies its local port in the constructor, we do not specify the local port in `UDPEchoClientTimeout.java`. How is the UDP echo client's socket given a port number? *Hint:* The answer is different for TCP.

chapter **3**

Sending and Receiving Data

Typically you use sockets because your program needs to provide information to, or use information provided by, another program. There is no magic: any programs that exchange information must agree on how that information will be *encoded*—represented as a sequence of bits—as well as which program sends what information when, and how the information received affects the behavior of the program. This agreement regarding the form and meaning of information exchanged over a communication channel is called a *protocol*; a protocol used in implementing a particular application is an *application protocol*. In our echo example from the earlier chapters, the application protocol is trivial: neither the client's nor the server's behavior is affected by the *contents* of the messages they exchange. Because in most real applications the behavior of clients and servers depends upon the information they exchange, application protocols are usually somewhat more complicated.

The TCP/IP protocols transport bytes of user data without examining or modifying them. This allows applications great flexibility in how they encode their information for transmission. Most application protocols are defined in terms of discrete *messages* made up of sequences of *fields*. Each field contains a specific piece of information encoded as a sequence of bits. The application protocol specifies exactly how these sequences of bits are to be arranged by the sender and interpreted, or *parsed*, by the receiver so that the latter can extract the meaning of each field. About the only constraint imposed by TCP/IP is that information must be sent and received in chunks whose length in bits is a multiple of eight. So from now on we consider messages to be sequences of *bytes*. Given this, it may be helpful to think of a transmitted message as a sequence or array of numbers, each between 0 and 255. That corresponds to the range of binary values that can be encoded in 8 bits: 00000000 for zero, 00000001 for one, 00000010 for two, and so on, up to 11111111 for 255.

When you build a program to exchange information via sockets with other programs, typically one of two situations applies: either you are designing/writing the programs on both sides of the socket, in which case you are free to define the application protocol yourself, or you are implementing a protocol that someone else has *already* specified, perhaps a protocol *standard*. In either case, the basic principles of encoding and decoding different types of information as bytes "on the wire" are the same. By the way, everything in this chapter also applies if the "wire" is a file that is written by one program and then read by another.

3.1   Encoding Information

Let's first consider the question of how simple values such as ints, longs, chars, and Strings can be sent and received via sockets. We have seen that bytes of information can be transmitted through a socket by writing them to an OutputStream (associated with a Socket) or encapsulating them in a DatagramPacket (which is then sent via a DatagramSocket). However, the only data types to which these operations can be applied are bytes and arrays of bytes. As a strongly typed language, Java requires that other types—int, String, and so on—be explicitly converted to byte arrays. Fortunately, the language has built-in facilities to help with such conversions. We saw one of these in Section 2.2.1: in TCPEchoClient.java, the getBytes() method of String, which converts the characters in a String instance to bytes in a standard way. Before considering the details of that kind of conversion, we first consider the representation of the most basic data types.

3.1.1   Primitive Integers

As we have already seen, TCP and UDP sockets give us the ability to send and receive sequences (arrays) of bytes, i.e., integer values in the range 0–255. Using that ability, we can encode the values of other (larger) primitive integer types. However, the sender and receiver have to agree on several things first. One is the *size* (in bytes) of each integer to be transmitted. For example, an int value in a Java program is represented as a 32-bit quantity. We can therefore transmit the value of any variable or constant of type int using four bytes. Values of type short, on the other hand, are represented using 16 bits and so only require two bytes to transmit, while longs are 64 bits or eight bytes.

Let's consider how we would encode a sequence of four integer values: a byte, a short, an int, and a long, in that order, for transmission from sender to receiver. We need a total of 15 bytes: the first contains the value of the byte, the next two contain the value of the short, the next four encode the value of the int, and the last eight bytes contain the long value, as shown below:

Are we ready to go? Not quite. For types that require more than one byte, we have to answer the question of which *order* to send the bytes in. There are two obvious choices: start at the right end of the integer, with the least significant byte—so-called *little-endian* order—or at the left end, with the most significant byte—*big-endian* order. (Note that the ordering of *bits within bytes* is, fortunately, handled by the implementation in a standard way.) Consider the long value 123456787654321L. Its 64-bit representation (in hexadecimal) is 0x0000704885F926B1. If we transmit the bytes in big-endian order, the sequence of (decimal) byte values will look like this:

0	0	112	72	133	249	38	177

order of transmission →

If we transmit them in little-endian order, the sequence will be:

177	38	249	133	72	112	0	0

order of transmission →

The main point is that for any multibyte integer quantity, the sender and receiver need to agree on whether big-endian or little-endian order will be used.[1] If the sender were to use little-endian order to send the above integer, and the receiver were expecting big-endian, instead of the correct value, the receiver would interpret the transmitted eight-byte sequence as the value 12765164544669515776L.

One last detail on which the sender and receiver must agree: whether the numbers transmitted will be *signed* or *unsigned*. The four primitive integer types in Java are all signed; values are stored in *two's-complement* representation, which is the usual way of representing signed numbers. When dealing with signed k-bit numbers, the two's-complement representation of the negative integer $-n$, $1 \leq n \leq 2^{k-1}$, is the binary value of $2^k - n$. The non-negative integer p, $0 \leq p \leq 2^{k-1} - 1$, is encoded simply by the k-bit binary value of p. Thus, given k bits, we can represent values in the range -2^{k-1} through $2^{k-1} - 1$ using two's-complement. Note that the most significant bit (msb) tells whether the value is positive (msb = 0) or negative (msb = 1). On the other hand, a k-bit, *unsigned* integer can encode values in the range 0 through $2^k - 1$ directly. So for example, the 32-bit value 0xFFFFFFFF (the all-ones value) when interpreted as a signed, two's complement integer represents -1; when interpreted as an unsigned integer,

---

[1] Java includes a class ByteOrder to denote these two possibilities. It has two static fields containing the (only) instances: ByteOrder.BIG_ENDIAN and ByteOrder.LITTLE_ENDIAN. Chapter 5 contains further details about this class.

it represents $4,294,967,295$. Because Java does not support unsigned integer types, encoding and decoding unsigned numbers in Java requires a little care. Assume for now that we are dealing with signed integer types.

So how do we get the correct values into the byte array of the message? To allow you to see exactly what needs to happen, here's how to do the encoding explicitly using "bit-diddling" (shifting and masking) operations. The program BruteForceCoding.java features a method encodeIntBigEndian() that can encode any value of one of the primitive types. Its arguments are the byte array into which the value is to be placed, the value to be encoded (represented as a long—which, as the largest type, can hold any of the other types), the offset in the array at which the value should start, and the size in bytes of the value to be written. If we encode at the sender, we must be able to decode at the receiver. BruteForceCoding also provides the decodeIntBigEndian() method for decoding a subset of a byte array into a Java long.

BruteForceCoding.java

```
0   public class BruteForceCoding {
1     private static byte byteVal = 101; // one hundred and one
2     private static short shortVal = 10001; // ten thousand and one
3     private static int intVal = 100000001; // one hundred million and one
4     private static long longVal = 1000000000001L;// one trillion and one
5
6     private final static int BSIZE = Byte.SIZE / Byte.SIZE;
7     private final static int SSIZE = Short.SIZE / Byte.SIZE;
8     private final static int ISIZE = Integer.SIZE / Byte.SIZE;
9     private final static int LSIZE = Long.SIZE / Byte.SIZE;
10
11    private final static int BYTEMASK = 0xFF; // 8 bits
12
13    public static String byteArrayToDecimalString(byte[] bArray) {
14      StringBuilder rtn = new StringBuilder();
15      for (byte b : bArray) {
16        rtn.append(b & BYTEMASK).append(" ");
17      }
18      return rtn.toString();
19    }
20
21    // Warning:  Untested preconditions (e.g., 0 <= size <= 8)
22    public static int encodeIntBigEndian(byte[] dst, long val, int offset, int size) {
23      for (int i = 0; i < size; i++) {
24        dst[offset++] = (byte) (val >> ((size - i - 1) * Byte.SIZE));
25      }
26      return offset;
27    }
```

```
28
29    // Warning:  Untested preconditions (e.g., 0 <= size <= 8)
30    public static long decodeIntBigEndian(byte[] val, int offset, int size) {
31      long rtn = 0;
32      for (int i = 0; i < size; i++) {
33        rtn = (rtn << Byte.SIZE) | ((long) val[offset + i] & BYTEMASK);
34      }
35      return rtn;
36    }
37
38    public static void main(String[] args) {
39      byte[] message = new byte[BSIZE + SSIZE + ISIZE + LSIZE];
40      // Encode the fields in the target byte array
41      int offset = encodeIntBigEndian(message, byteVal, 0, BSIZE);
42      offset = encodeIntBigEndian(message, shortVal, offset, SSIZE);
43      offset = encodeIntBigEndian(message, intVal, offset, ISIZE);
44      encodeIntBigEndian(message, longVal, offset, LSIZE);
45      System.out.println("Encoded message: " + byteArrayToDecimalString(message));
46
47      // Decode several fields
48      long value = decodeIntBigEndian(message, BSIZE, SSIZE);
49      System.out.println("Decoded short = " + value);
50      value = decodeIntBigEndian(message, BSIZE + SSIZE + ISIZE, LSIZE);
51      System.out.println("Decoded long = " + value);
52
53      // Demonstrate dangers of conversion
54      offset = 4;
55      value = decodeIntBigEndian(message, offset, BSIZE);
56      System.out.println("Decoded value (offset " + offset + ", size " + BSIZE + ") = "
57          + value);
58      byte bVal = (byte) decodeIntBigEndian(message, offset, BSIZE);
59      System.out.println("Same value as byte = " + bVal);
60    }
61
62  }
```

BruteForceCoding.java

1. **Data items to encode:** lines 1–4

2. **Numbers of bytes in Java integer primitives:** lines 6–9

3. byteArrayToDecimalString(): lines 13–19
    This method prints each byte from the given array as an unsigned decimal value.
    BYTEMASK keeps the byte value from being *sign-extended* when it is converted to an int
    in the call to append(), thus rendering it as an unsigned integer.

4. `encodeIntBigEndian()`: lines 22-27
   The right-hand side of the assignment statement first shifts the value to the right so the byte we are interested in is in the low-order eight bits. The resulting value is then *cast* to the type byte, which throws away all but the low-order eight bits, and placed in the array at the appropriate location. This is iterated over size bytes of the given value, `val`. The new offset is returned so we need not keep track of it.

5. `decodeIntBigEndian()`: lines 30-36
   Iterate over size bytes of the given array, accumulating the result in a `long`, which is shifted left at each iteration.

6. **Demonstrate methods:** lines 38-60
   - **Prepare array to receive series of integers:** line 39
   - **Encode items:** lines 40-44
     The `byte`, `short`, `int`, and `long` are encoded into the array in the sequence described earlier.
   - **Print contents of encoded array:** line 45
   - **Decode several fields from encoded byte array:** lines 47-51
     Output should show the decoded values equal to the original constants.
   - **Conversion problems:** lines 53-59
     At offset 4, the byte value is 245 (decimal); however, when read as a *signed* byte value, it should be −11 (recall two's-complement representation of signed integers). If we place the return value into a long, it simply becomes the last byte of a long, producing a value of 245. Placing the return value into a byte yields a value of −11. Which answer is correct depends on your application. If you expect a signed value from decoding N bytes, you must place the (long) result in a primitive integer type that uses exactly N bytes. If you expect an unsigned value from decoding N bytes, you must place the results in a primitive integer type that uses at least $N + 1$ bytes.

Note that there are several preconditions we might consider testing at the beginning of `encodeIntBigEndian()` and `decodeIntBigEndian()`, such as $0 \leq size \leq 8$ and $dst \neq null$. Can you name any others?

Running the program produces output showing the following (decimal) byte values:

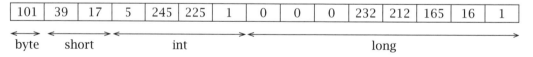

| 101 | 39 | 17 | 5 | 245 | 225 | 1 | 0 | 0 | 0 | 232 | 212 | 165 | 16 | 1 |

byte   short   int   long

As you can see, the brute-force method requires the programmer to do quite a bit of work: computing and naming the offset and size of each value, and invoking the encoding routine with the appropriate arguments. It would be even worse if the `encodeIntBigEndian()` method were not factored out as a separate method. For that reason, it is not the recommended approach, because Java provides some built-in mechanisms that are easier to use. Note that it does have the advantage that, in addition to the standard Java integer sizes, encodeIntegerBigEndian() works with *any* size integer from 1 to 8 bytes—for example, you can encode a seven-byte integer if you like.

A relatively easy way to construct the message in this example is to use the Data-OutputStream and ByteArrayOutputStream classes. The DataOutputStream allows you to write primitive types like the integers we've been discussing to a stream: it provides writeByte(), writeShort(), writeInt(), and writeLong() methods, which take an integer value and write it to the stream in the appropriately sized big-endian two's-complement representation. The ByteArrayOutputStream class takes the sequence of bytes written to a stream and converts it to a byte array. The code for building our message looks like this:

```
ByteArrayOutputStream buf = new ByteArrayOutputStream();
DataOutputStream out = new DataOutputStream(buf);
out.writeByte(byteVal);
out.writeShort(shortVal);
out.writeInt(intVal);
out.writeLong(longVal);
out.flush();
byte[] msg = buf.toByteArray();
```

You may want to run this code to convince yourself that it produces the same output as BruteForceEncoding.java.

So much for the sending side. How does the receiver recover the transmitted values? As you might expect, there are input analogues for the output facilities we used, namely DataInput-Stream and ByteArrayInputStream. We'll show an example of their use later, when we discuss how to parse incoming messages. Also, in Chapter 5, we'll see another way of converting primitive types to byte sequences, using the ByteBuffer class.

Finally, essentially everything in this subsection applies also to the BigInteger class, which supports arbitrarily large integers. As with the primitive integer types, sender and receiver have to agree on a specific size (number of bytes) to represent the value. However, this defeats the purpose of using a BigInteger, which can be arbitrarily large. One approach is to use length-based framing, which we'll see in Section 3.3.

3.1.2 Strings and Text

Old-fashioned *text*—strings of printable (displayable) characters—is perhaps the most common way to represent information. Text is convenient because humans are accustomed to dealing with all kinds of information represented as strings of characters in books, newspapers, and on computer displays. Thus, once we know how to encode text for transmission, we can send almost any other kind of data: first represent it as text, then encode the text. Obviously we can represent numbers and boolean values as Strings—for example "123478962", "6.02e23", "true", "false". And we've already seen that a string can be converted to a byte array by calling the getBytes() method (see TCPEchoClient.java). Alas, there is more to it than that.

To better understand what's going on, we first need to consider that text is made up of symbols or *characters*. In fact every String instance corresponds to a sequence (array) of *characters* (type char[ ]). A char value in Java is represented internally as an integer. For example, the character "a", that is, the symbol for the letter "a", corresponds to the integer 97. The character "X" corresponds to 88, and the symbol "!" (exclamation mark) corresponds to 33.

A mapping between a set of symbols and a set of integers is called a *coded character set*. You may have heard of the coded character set known as *ASCII—American Standard Code for Information Interchange*. ASCII maps the letters of the English alphabet, digits, punctuation and some other special (non-printable) symbols to integers between 0 and 127. It has been used for data transmission since the 1960s, and is used extensively in application protocols such as HTTP (the protocol used for the World Wide Web), even today. However, because it omits symbols used by many languages other than English, it is less than ideal for developing applications and protocols designed to function in today's global economy.

Java therefore uses an international standard coded character set called *Unicode* to represent values of type char and String. Unicode maps symbols from "most of the languages and symbol systems of the world" [19] to integers between 0 and 65,535, and is much better suited for internationalized programs. For example, the Japanese Hiragana symbol for the syllable "o" maps to the integer 12,362. Unicode includes ASCII: each symbol defined by ASCII maps to the same integer in Unicode as it does in ASCII. This provides a degree of backward compatibility between ASCII and Unicode.

So sender and receiver have to agree on a mapping from symbols to integers in order to communicate using text messages. Is that all they need to agree on? It depends. For a small set of characters with no integer value larger than 255, nothing more is needed because each character can be encoded as a single byte. For a code that may use larger integer values that require more than a single byte to represent, there is more than one way to encode those values on the wire. Thus, sender and receiver need to agree on how those integers will be represented as byte sequences—that is, an *encoding scheme*. The combination of a coded character set and a character encoding scheme is called a *charset* (see RFC 2278). It is possible to define your own charset, but there is hardly ever a reason to do so. A large number of different *standardized* charsets are in use around the world. Java provides support for the use of arbitrary charsets, and every implementation is required to support at least the following: US-ASCII (another name for ASCII), ISO-8859-1, UTF-8, UTF-16BE, UTF-16LE, UTF-16.

When you invoke the getBytes() method of a String instance, it returns a byte array containing the String encoded according to the *default charset* for the platform. On many platforms the default charset is UTF-8; however, in localities that make frequent use of characters outside the ASCII charset, it may be something different. To ensure that a string is encoded using a *particular* charset, you simply supply the name of the charset as a (String) argument to the getBytes() method. The resulting byte array contains the representation of the string in the given encoding. (Note that in the example TCP Echo Client/Server from Section 2.2.1 the encoding was *irrelevant* because the server did not interpret the received data at all.)

For example, if you call "Test!".getBytes() on the platform on which this book was written, you get back the encoding according to UTF-8: If you call "Test!".getBytes("UTF-16BE"), on

84	101	115	116	33

the other hand, you get the following array: In this case each value is encoded as a two-byte

0	84	0	101	0	115	0	116	0	33

sequence, with the high-order byte first. From "Test!".getBytes("IBM037"), the result is:

227	133	162	163	90

The moral of the story is that *sender and receiver must agree on the representation for strings of text*. The easiest way for them to do that is to simply specify one of the standard charsets.

As we have seen, it is possible to write Strings to an OutputStream by first converting them individually to bytes and then writing the result to the stream. That method requires that the encoding be specified on every call to getBytes(). Later in the chapter we'll see a way to simply specify the encoding once when constructing text messages.

3.1.3 Bit-Diddling: Encoding Booleans

Bitmaps are a very compact way to encode boolean information, which is often used in protocols. The idea of a bitmap is that each of the bits of an integer type can encode one boolean value—typically with 0 representing false, and 1 representing true. To be able to manipulate bitmaps, you need to know how to set and clear individual bits using Java's "bit-diddling" operations. A *mask* is an integer value that has one or more specific bits set to 1, and all others cleared (i.e., 0). We'll deal here mainly with int-sized bitmaps and masks (32 bits), but everything we say applies to other integer types as well.

Let's number the bits of a value of type int from 0 to 31, where bit 0 is the least significant bit. In general, the int value that has a 1 in bit position i, and a zero in all other bit positions, is just 2^i. So bit 5 is represented by 32, bit 12 by 4096, etc. Here are some example mask declarations:

```
final int BIT5 = (1<<5);
final int BIT7 = 0x80;
final int BITS2AND3 = 12;    // 8+4
int bitmap = 1234567;
```

To *set* a particular bit in an int variable, combine it with the mask for that bit using the bitwise-OR operation (|):

```
bitmap |= BIT5;
// bit 5 is now one
```

To *clear* a particular bit, bitwise-AND it with the *bitwise complement* of the mask for that bit (which has ones everywhere except the particular bit, which is zero). The bitwise-AND operation in Java is &, while the bitwise-complement operator is ~.

```
bitmap &= ~BIT7;
// bit 7 is now zero
```

You can set and clear multiple bits at once by OR-ing together the corresponding masks:

```
// clear bits 2, 3 and 5
bitmap &= ~(BITS2AND3|BIT5);
```

To test whether a bit is set, compare the result of the bitwise-AND of the mask and the value with zero:

```
boolean bit6Set = (bitmap & (1<<6)) != 0;
```

3.2   Composing I/O Streams

Java's stream classes can be composed to provide powerful capabilities. For example, we can wrap the OutputStream of a Socket instance in a BufferedOutputStream instance to improve performance by buffering bytes temporarily and flushing them to the underlying channel all at once. We can then wrap that instance in a DataOutputStream to send primitive data types. We would code this composition as follows:

```
Socket socket = new Socket(server, port);
DataOutputStream out = new DataOutputStream(
    new BufferedOutputStream(socket.getOutputStream()));
```

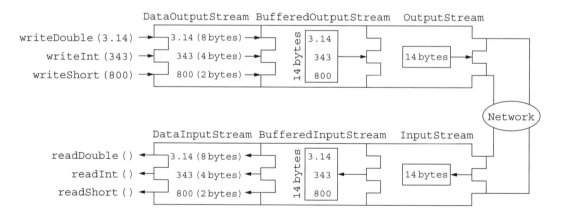

Figure 3.1: Stream composition.

I/O Class	Function
Buffered[Input/Output]Stream	Performs buffering for I/O optimization.
Checked[Input/Output]Stream	Maintains a checksum on data.
Cipher[Input/Output]Stream	Encrypt/Decrypt data.
Data[Input/Output]Stream	Handles read/write for primitive date types.
Digest[Input/Output]Stream	Maintains a digest on data.
GZIP[Input/Output]Stream	De/compresses a byte stream in GZIP format.
Object[Input/Output]Stream	Handles read/write objects and primitive data types.
PushbackInputStream	Allows a byte or bytes to be "unread."
PrintOutputStream	Prints string representation of data type.
Zip[Input/Output]Stream	De/compresses a byte stream in ZIP format.

Table 3.1: Java I/O Classes

Figure 3.1 demonstrates this composition. Here, we write our primitive data values, one by one, to DataOutputStream, which writes the binary data to BufferedOutputStream, which buffers the data from the three writes and then writes once to the socket OutputStream, which controls writing to the network. We create a corresponding composition for the InputStream on the other endpoint to efficiently receive primitive data types.

A complete description of the Java I/O API is beyond the scope of this text; however, Table 3.1 provides a list of some of the relevant Java I/O classes as a starting point for exploiting its capabilities.

3.3 Framing and Parsing

Converting data to wire format is, of course, only half the story; the original information must be recovered at the receiver from the transmitted sequence of bytes. Application protocols typically deal with discrete messages, which are viewed as collections of fields. *Framing* refers to the problem of enabling the receiver to locate the beginning and end of a message. Whether information is encoded as text, as multibyte binary numbers, or as some combination of the two, the application protocol must specify how the receiver of a message can determine when it has received all of the message.

Of course, if a complete message is sent as the payload of a DatagramPacket, the problem is trivial: the payload of the DatagramPacket has a definite length, and the receiver knows exactly where the message ends. For messages sent over TCP sockets, however, the situation can be more complicated because TCP has no notion of message boundaries. If the fields in a message all have fixed sizes and the message is made up of a fixed number of fields, then the size of the message is known in advance and the receiver can simply read the expected number of bytes into a `byte[]` buffer. This technique was used in `TCPEchoClient.java`, where we knew the number of bytes to expect from the server. However, when the message can vary in length—for example, if it contains some variable-length arbitrary text strings—we do not know beforehand how many bytes to read.

If a receiver tries to receive more bytes from the socket than were in the message, one of two things can happen. If no other message is in the channel, the receiver will block and be prevented from processing the message; if the sender is also blocked waiting for a reply, the result will be *deadlock*. On the other hand, if another message is in the channel, the receiver may read some or all of it as part of the first message, leading to protocol errors. Therefore framing is an important consideration when using TCP sockets.

Note that some of the same considerations apply to finding the boundaries of the individual *fields* of the message: the receiver needs to know where one ends and another begins. Thus, pretty much everything we say here about framing messages also applies to fields. However, it is simplest, and also leads to the cleanest code, if you deal with these two problems separately: first locate the end of the message, then parse the message as a whole. Here we focus on framing complete messages.

Two general techniques enable a receiver to unambiguously find the end of the message:

- *Delimiter-based*: The end of the message is indicated by a *unique marker*, an explicit byte sequence that the sender transmits immediately following the data. The marker must be known not to occur in the data.

- *Explicit length*: The variable-length field or message is preceded by a (fixed-size) length field that tells how many bytes it contains.

A special case of the delimiter-based method can be used for the last message sent on a TCP connection: the sender simply closes the sending side of the connection (using `shutdownOutput()` or `close()`) after sending the message. After the receiver reads the last byte of the message, it receives an end-of-stream indication (i.e., `read()` returns -1), and thus can tell that it has reached the end of the message.

The delimiter-based approach is often used with messages encoded as text: A particular character or sequence of characters is defined to mark the end of the message. The receiver simply scans the input (as characters) looking for the delimiter sequence; it returns the character string preceding the delimiter. The drawback is that *the message itself must not contain the delimiter*, otherwise the receiver will find the end of the message prematurely. With a delimiter-based framing method, the sender is responsible for ensuring that this precondition is satisfied. Fortunately so-called *stuffing* techniques allow delimiters that occur naturally in the message to be modified so the receiver will not recognize them as such; as it scans for the delimiter, it also recognizes the modified delimiters and restores them in the output message so it matches the original. The downside of such techniques is that *both* sender and receiver have to scan the message.

The length-based approach is simpler, but requires a known upper bound on the size of the message. The sender first determines the length of the message, encodes it as an integer, and prefixes the result to the message. The upper bound on the message length determines the number of bytes required to encode the length: one byte if messages always contain fewer than 256 bytes, two bytes if they are always shorter than 65,536 bytes, and so on.

In order to demonstrate these techniques, we introduce the interface Framer, which is defined below. It has two methods: frameMsg() adds framing information and outputs a given message to a given stream, while nextMsg() scans a given stream, extracting the next message.

Framer.java

```
0  import java.io.IOException;
1  import java.io.OutputStream;
2
3  public interface Framer {
4    void frameMsg(byte[] message, OutputStream out) throws IOException;
5    byte[] nextMsg() throws IOException;
6  }
```

Framer.java

The class DelimFramer.java implements delimiter-based framing using the "newline" character ("\n", byte value 10). The frameMethod() method does *not* do stuffing, but simply throws an exception if the byte sequence to be framed contains the delimiter. (Extending the method to do stuffing is left as an excercise.) The nextMsg() method scans the stream until it reads the delimiter, then returns everything up to the delimiter; NULL is returned if the stream is empty. If some bytes of a message are accumulated and the stream ends without finding a delimiter, an exception is thrown to indicate a framing error.

DelimFramer.java

```
0   import java.io.ByteArrayOutputStream;
1   import java.io.EOFException;
2   import java.io.IOException;
3   import java.io.InputStream;
4   import java.io.OutputStream;
5
6   public class DelimFramer implements Framer {
7
8     private InputStream in;        // data source
9     private static final byte DELIMITER = "\n"; // message delimiter
10
```

```
11    public DelimFramer(InputStream in) {
12      this.in = in;
13    }
14
15    public void frameMsg(byte[] message, OutputStream out) throws IOException {
16      // ensure that the message does not contain the delimiter
17      for (byte b : message) {
18        if (b == DELIMITER) {
19          throw new IOException("Message contains delimiter");
20        }
21      }
22      out.write(message);
23      out.write(DELIMITER);
24      out.flush();
25    }
26
27    public byte[] nextMsg() throws IOException {
28      ByteArrayOutputStream messageBuffer = new ByteArrayOutputStream();
29      int nextByte;
30
31      // fetch bytes until find delimiter
32      while ((nextByte = in.read()) != DELIMITER) {
33        if (nextByte == -1) { // end of stream?
34          if (messageBuffer.size() == 0) { // if no byte read
35            return null;
36          } else { // if bytes followed by end of stream: framing error
37            throw new EOFException("Non-empty message without delimiter");
38          }
39        }
40        messageBuffer.write(nextByte); // write byte to buffer
41      }
42
43      return messageBuffer.toByteArray();
44    }
45  }
```

DelimFramer.java

1. **Constructor:** lines 11–13
   The input stream from which messages are to be extracted is given as an argument.

2. frameMsg() **adds framing information:** lines 15–25
   - **Verify well-formedness:** lines 17–21
     Check that the given message does not contain the delimiter; if so, throw an exception.

- **Write message:** line 22
  Output the framed message to the stream
- **Write delimiter:** line 23

3. nextMsg() **extracts messages from input:** lines 27–44
   - **Read each byte in the stream until the delimiter is found:** line 32
   - **Handle end of stream:** lines 33–39
     If the end of stream occurs before finding the delimiter, throw an exception if any bytes have been read since construction of the framer or the last delimiter; otherwise return NULL to indicate that all messages have been received.
   - **Write non-delimiter byte to message buffer:** line 40
   - **Return contents of message buffer as byte array:** line 43

There's a limitation to our delimiting framer: it does not support multibyte delimiters. We leave fixing this as an exercise for the reader.

The class LengthFramer.java implements length-based framing for messages up to 65,535 ($2^{16} - 1$) bytes in length. The sender determines the length of the given message and writes it to the output stream as a two-byte, big-endian integer, followed by the complete message. On the receiving side, we use a DataInputStream to be able to read the length as an integer; the readFully() method blocks until the given array is completely full, which is exactly what we need here. Note that, with this framing method, the sender does not have to inspect the content of the message being framed; it needs only to check that the message does not exceed the length limit.

LengthFramer.java

```
0   import java.io.DataInputStream;
1   import java.io.EOFException;
2   import java.io.IOException;
3   import java.io.InputStream;
4   import java.io.OutputStream;
5
6   public class LengthFramer implements Framer {
7     public static final int MAXMESSAGELENGTH = 65535;
8     public static final int BYTEMASK = 0xff;
9     public static final int SHORTMASK = 0xffff;
10    public static final int BYTESHIFT = 8;
11
12    private DataInputStream in; // wrapper for data I/O
13
14    public LengthFramer(InputStream in) throws IOException {
15      this.in = new DataInputStream(in);
16    }
17
```

```
18    public void frameMsg(byte[] message, OutputStream out) throws IOException {
19      if (message.length > MAXMESSAGELENGTH) {
20        throw new IOException("message too long");
21      }
22      // write length prefix
23      out.write((message.length >> BYTESHIFT) & BYTEMASK);
24      out.write(message.length & BYTEMASK);
25      // write message
26      out.write(message);
27      out.flush();
28    }
29
30    public byte[] nextMsg() throws IOException {
31      int length;
32      try {
33        length = in.readUnsignedShort(); // read 2 bytes
34      } catch (EOFException e) { // no (or 1 byte) message
35        return null;
36      }
37      // 0 <= length <= 65535
38      byte[] msg = new byte[length];
39      in.readFully(msg); // if exception, it's a framing error.
40      return msg;
41    }
42  }
```

LengthFramer.java

1. **Constructor:** lines 14–16
   Take the input stream source for framed messages and wrap it in a DataInputStream.

2. frameMsg() **adds framing information:** lines 18–28
   - **Verify length:** lines 19–21
     Because we use a two-byte length field, the length cannot exceed 65,535. (Note that this value is too big to store in a short, so we write it a byte at a time.)
   - **Output length field:** lines 23–24
     Output the message bytes prefixed by the length (unsigned short).
   - **Output message:** line 26

3. nextMsg() **extracts next frame from input:** lines 30–41
   - **Read the prefix length:** lines 32–36
     The readUnsignedShort() method reads two bytes, interprets them as a big-endian integer, and returns their value as an int.

- **Read the specified number of bytes:** lines 38–39
  The readfully() method blocks until enough bytes to fill the given array have been returned.
- **Return bytes as message:** line 40

3.4 Java-Specific Encodings

When you use sockets, generally either you are building the programs on both ends of the communication channel—in which case you also have complete control over the protocol—or you are communicating using a *given* protocol, which you have to implement. When you know that (i) both ends of the communication will be implemented in Java, and (ii) you have complete control over the protocol, you can make use of Java's built-in facilities like the Serializable interface or the *Remote Method Invocation (RMI)* facility. RMI lets you invoke methods on different Java virtual machines, hiding all the messy details of argument encoding and decoding. Serialization handles conversion of actual Java objects to byte sequences for you, so you can transfer actual instances of Java objects between virtual machines.

These capabilities might seem like communication Nirvana, but in reality they are not always the best solution, for several reasons. First, because they are very general facilities, they are not the most efficient in terms of communication overhead. For example, the serialized form of an object generally includes information that is meaningless outside the context of the Java Virtual Machine (JVM). Second, Serializable and Externalizable cannot be used when a different wire format has already been specified—for example, by a standardized protocol. And finally, custom-designed classes have to provide their own implementations of the serialization interfaces, *and this is not easy to get right*. Again, there are certainly situations where these built-in facilities are useful; but sometimes it is simpler, easier, or more efficient to "roll your own."

3.5 Constructing and Parsing Protocol Messages

We close this chapter with a simple example to illustrate some techniques you might use to implement a protocol specified by someone else. The example is a simple "voting" protocol as shown in Figure 3.2. Here a client sends a request message to a server; the message contains

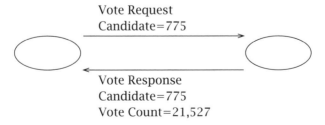

Figure 3.2: Voting protocol.

a candidate ID, which is an integer between 0 and 1000. Two types of requests are supported. An *inquiry* asks the server how many votes have been cast for the given candidate. The server sends back a response message containing the original candidate ID and the vote total (as of the time the request was received) for that candidate. A *voting* request actually casts a vote for the indicated candidate. The server again responds with a message containing the candidate ID and the vote total (which now includes the vote just cast).

In implementing a protocol, it is helpful to define a class to contain the information carried in a message. The class provides methods for manipulating the fields of the message—while maintaining the invariants that are supposed to hold among those fields. For our simple example, the messages sent by client and server are very similar. The only difference is that the messages sent by the server contain the vote count and a flag indicating that they are responses (not requests). In this case, we can get away with a single class for both kinds of messages. The VoteMsg.java class shows the basic information in each message:

- a boolean *isInquiry*, which is true if the requested transaction is an inquiry (and false if it is an actual vote);

- a boolean *isResponse* indicating whether the message is a response (sent by the server) or request;

- an integer *candidateID* that identifies the candidate;

- a long *voteCount* indicating the vote total for the requested candidate

The class maintains the following invariants among the fields:

- *candidateID* is in the range 0–1000.

- *voteCount* is only nonzero in response messages (*isResponse* is true).

- *voteCount* is non-negative.

VoteMsg.java

```
0   public class VoteMsg {
1     private boolean isInquiry;  // true if inquiry; false if vote
2     private boolean isResponse;// true if response from server
3     private int candidateID;    // in [0,1000]
4     private long voteCount;     // nonzero only in response
5
6     public static final int MAX_CANDIDATE_ID = 1000;
7
8     public VoteMsg(boolean isResponse, boolean isInquiry, int candidateID, long voteCount)
9         throws IllegalArgumentException {
10      // check invariants
11      if (voteCount != 0 && !isResponse) {
12        throw new IllegalArgumentException("Request vote count must be zero");
```

```
13        }
14        if (candidateID < 0 || candidateID > MAX_CANDIDATE_ID) {
15          throw new IllegalArgumentException("Bad Candidate ID: " + candidateID);
16        }
17        if (voteCount < 0) {
18          throw new IllegalArgumentException("Total must be >= zero");
19        }
20        this.candidateID = candidateID;
21        this.isResponse = isResponse;
22        this.isInquiry = isInquiry;
23        this.voteCount = voteCount;
24      }
25
26      public void setInquiry(boolean isInquiry) {
27        this.isInquiry = isInquiry;
28      }
29
30      public void setResponse(boolean isResponse) {
31        this.isResponse = isResponse;
32      }
33
34      public boolean isInquiry() {
35        return isInquiry;
36      }
37
38      public boolean isResponse() {
39        return isResponse;
40      }
41
42      public void setCandidateID(int candidateID) throws IllegalArgumentException {
43        if (candidateID < 0 || candidateID > MAX_CANDIDATE_ID) {
44          throw new IllegalArgumentException("Bad Candidate ID: " + candidateID);
45        }
46        this.candidateID = candidateID;
47      }
48
49      public int getCandidateID() {
50        return candidateID;
51      }
52
53      public void setVoteCount(long count) {
54        if ((count != 0 && !isResponse) || count < 0) {
55          throw new IllegalArgumentException("Bad vote count");
56        }
57        voteCount = count;
```

```
58     }
59
60     public long getVoteCount() {
61       return voteCount;
62     }
63
64     public String toString() {
65       String res = (isInquiry ? "inquiry" : "vote") + " for candidate " + candidateID;
66       if (isResponse) {
67         res = "response to " + res + " who now has " + voteCount + " vote(s)";
68       }
69       return res;
70     }
71   }
```

VoteMsg.java

Now that we have a Java representation of a vote message, we need some way to encode and decode according to some protocol. A VoteMsgCoder provides the methods for vote message serialization and deserialization.

VoteMsgCoder.java

```
0   import java.io.IOException;
1
2   public interface VoteMsgCoder {
3     byte[] toWire(VoteMsg msg) throws IOException;
4     VoteMsg fromWire(byte[] input) throws IOException;
5   }
```

VoteMsgCoder.java

The toWire() method converts the vote message to a sequence of bytes according to a particular protocol, and the fromWire() method parses a given sequence of bytes according to the same protocol and constructs an instance of the message class.

To illustrate the different methods of encoding information, we present two implementations of VoteMsgCoder, one using a text-based encoding and one using a binary encoding. If you were guaranteed a single encoding that would never change, the toWire() and fromWire() methods could be specified as part of VoteMsg. Our purpose here is to emphasize that the abstract representation is independent of the details of the encoding.

3.5.1 Text-Based Representation

We first present a version in which messages are encoded as text. The protocol specifies that the text be encoded using the US-ASCII charset. The message begins with a so-called "magic string"—a sequence of characters that allows a recipient to quickly recognize the message as a Voting protocol message, as opposed to random garbage that happened to arrive over the network. The Vote/Inquiry boolean is encoded with the character 'v' for a vote or 'i' for an inquiry. The message's status as a response is indicated by the presence of the character 'R'. Then comes the candidate ID, followed by the vote count, both encoded as decimal strings. The VoteMsgTextCoder provides a text-based encoding of VoteMsg.

VoteMsgTextCoder.java

```
0   import java.io.ByteArrayInputStream;
1   import java.io.IOException;
2   import java.io.InputStreamReader;
3   import java.util.Scanner;
4
5   public class VoteMsgTextCoder implements VoteMsgCoder {
6     /*
7      * Wire Format "VOTEPROTO" <"v"|"i"> [<RESPFLAG>] <CANDIDATE> [<VOTECNT>]
8      * Charset is fixed by the wire format.
9      */
10
11    // Manifest constants for encoding
12    public static final String MAGIC = "Voting";
13    public static final String VOTESTR = "v";
14    public static final String INQSTR = "i";
15    public static final String RESPONSESTR = "R";
16
17    public static final String CHARSETNAME = "US-ASCII";
18    public static final String DELIMSTR = " ";
19    public static final int MAX_WIRE_LENGTH = 2000;
20
21    public byte[] toWire(VoteMsg msg) throws IOException {
22      String msgString = MAGIC + DELIMSTR + (msg.isInquiry() ? INQSTR : VOTESTR)
23          + DELIMSTR + (msg.isResponse() ? RESPONSESTR + DELIMSTR : "")
24          + Integer.toString(msg.getCandidateID()) + DELIMSTR
25          + Long.toString(msg.getVoteCount());
26      byte data[] = msgString.getBytes(CHARSETNAME);
27      return data;
28    }
29
30    public VoteMsg fromWire(byte[] message) throws IOException {
31      ByteArrayInputStream msgStream = new ByteArrayInputStream(message);
32      Scanner s = new Scanner(new InputStreamReader(msgStream, CHARSETNAME));
33      boolean isInquiry;
34      boolean isResponse;
35      int candidateID;
36      long voteCount;
```

```
37      String token;
38
39      try {
40        token = s.next();
41        if (!token.equals(MAGIC)) {
42          throw new IOException("Bad magic string: " + token);
43        }
44        token = s.next();
45        if (token.equals(VOTESTR)) {
46          isInquiry = false;
47        } else if (!token.equals(INQSTR)) {
48          throw new IOException("Bad vote/inq indicator: " + token);
49        } else {
50          isInquiry = true;
51        }
52
53        token = s.next();
54        if (token.equals(RESPONSESTR)) {
55          isResponse = true;
56          token = s.next();
57        } else {
58          isResponse = false;
59        }
60        // Current token is candidateID
61        // Note: isResponse now valid
62        candidateID = Integer.parseInt(token);
63        if (isResponse) {
64          token = s.next();
65          voteCount = Long.parseLong(token);
66        } else {
67          voteCount = 0;
68        }
69      } catch (IOException ioe) {
70        throw new IOException("Parse error...");
71      }
72      return new VoteMsg(isResponse, isInquiry, candidateID, voteCount);
73    }
74  }
```

_____

VoteMsgTextCoder.java

The toWire() method simply constructs a string containing all the fields of the message, separated by white space. The fromWire() method first looks for the "Magic" string; if it is not the first thing in the message, it throws an exception. This illustrates a very important point about implementing protocols: *never assume anything about any input from the network.*

Your program must always be prepared for any possible inputs, and handle them gracefully. In this case, the fromWire() method throws an exception if the expected string is not present. Otherwise, it gets the fields token by token, using the Scanner instance. Note that the number of fields in the message depends on whether it is a request (sent by the client) or response (sent by the server). fromWire() throws an exception if the input ends prematurely or is otherwise malformed.

3.5.2   Binary Representation

Next we present a different way to encode the Voting protocol message. In contrast with the text-based format, the binary format uses fixed-size messages. Each message begins with a one-byte field that contains the "magic" value 010101 in its high-order six bits. This little bit of redundancy provides the receiver with a small degree of assurance that it is receiving a proper voting message. The two low-order bits of the first byte encode the two booleans. The second byte of the message always contains zeros, and the third and fourth bytes contain the candidateID. The final eight bytes of a response message (only) contain the vote count.

VoteMsgBinCoder.java

```
0   import java.io.ByteArrayInputStream;
1   import java.io.ByteArrayOutputStream;
2   import java.io.DataInputStream;
3   import java.io.DataOutputStream;
4   import java.io.IOException;
5
6   /* Wire Format
7    *                               1  1  1  1  1  1
8    *   0  1  2  3  4  5  6  7  8  9  0  1  2  3  4  5
9    * +--+--+--+--+--+--+--+--+--+--+--+--+--+--+--+--+
10   * |     Magic        |Flags|        ZERO          |
11   * +--+--+--+--+--+--+--+--+--+--+--+--+--+--+--+--+
12   * |                 Candidate ID                  |
13   * +--+--+--+--+--+--+--+--+--+--+--+--+--+--+--+--+
14   * |                                               |
15   * |          Vote Count (only in response)        |
16   * |                                               |
17   * |                                               |
18   * +--+--+--+--+--+--+--+--+--+--+--+--+--+--+--+--+
19   */
20  public class VoteMsgBinCoder implements VoteMsgCoder {
21
22      // manifest constants for encoding
23      public static final int MIN_WIRE_LENGTH = 4;
24      public static final int MAX_WIRE_LENGTH = 16;
```

```
25    public static final int MAGIC = 0x5400;
26    public static final int MAGIC_MASK = 0xfc00;
27    public static final int MAGIC_SHIFT = 8;
28    public static final int RESPONSE_FLAG = 0x0200;
29    public static final int INQUIRE_FLAG =  0x0100;
30
31    public byte[] toWire(VoteMsg msg) throws IOException {
32      ByteArrayOutputStream byteStream = new ByteArrayOutputStream();
33      DataOutputStream out = new DataOutputStream(byteStream); // converts ints
34
35      short magicAndFlags = MAGIC;
36      if (msg.isInquiry()) {
37        magicAndFlags |= INQUIRE_FLAG;
38      }
39      if (msg.isResponse()) {
40        magicAndFlags |= RESPONSE_FLAG;
41      }
42      out.writeShort(magicAndFlags);
43      // We know the candidate ID will fit in a short: it's > 0 && < 1000
44      out.writeShort((short) msg.getCandidateID());
45      if (msg.isResponse()) {
46        out.writeLong(msg.getVoteCount());
47      }
48      out.flush();
49      byte[] data = byteStream.toByteArray();
50      return data;
51    }
52
53    public VoteMsg fromWire(byte[] input) throws IOException {
54      // sanity checks
55      if (input.length < MIN_WIRE_LENGTH) {
56        throw new IOException("Runt message");
57      }
58      ByteArrayInputStream bs = new ByteArrayInputStream(input);
59      DataInputStream in = new DataInputStream(bs);
60      int magic = in.readShort();
61      if ((magic & MAGIC_MASK) != MAGIC) {
62        throw new IOException("Bad Magic #: " +
63                              ((magic & MAGIC_MASK) >> MAGIC_SHIFT));
64      }
65      boolean resp = ((magic & RESPONSE_FLAG) != 0);
66      boolean inq = ((magic & INQUIRE_FLAG) != 0);
67      int candidateID = in.readShort();
68      if (candidateID < 0 || candidateID > 1000) {
69        throw new IOException("Bad candidate ID: " + candidateID);
```

```
70        }
71        long count = 0;
72        if (resp) {
73          count = in.readLong();
74          if (count < 0) {
75            throw new IOException("Bad vote count: " + count);
76          }
77        }
78        // Ignore any extra bytes
79        return new VoteMsg(resp, inq, candidateID, count);
80      }
81    }
```

VoteMsgBinCoder.java

As in Section 3.1.1, we create a ByteArrayOutputStream and wrap it in a DataOutputStream to receive the result. The encoding method takes advantage of the fact that the high-order two bytes of a valid candidateID are always zero. Note also the use of bitwise-or operations to encode the booleans using a single bit each.

3.5.3 Sending and Receiving

Sending a message over a stream is as simple as creating it, calling toWire(), adding appropriate framing information, and writing it. Receiving, of course, does things in the opposite order. This approach applies to TCP; in UDP explicit framing is not necessary, because message boundaries are preserved. To demonstrate this, consider a vote server that 1) maintains a mapping of candidate IDs to number of votes, 2) counts submitted votes, and 3) responds to inquiries and votes with the current count for the specified candidate. We begin by implementing a service for use by vote servers. When a vote server receives a vote message, it handles the request by calling the handleRequest() method of VoteService.

VoteService.java

```
0   import java.util.HashMap;
1   import java.util.Map;
2
3   public class VoteService {
4
5     // Map of candidates to number of votes
6     private Map<Integer, Long> results = new HashMap<Integer, Long>();
7
8     public VoteMsg handleRequest(VoteMsg msg) {
9       if (msg.isResponse()) { // If response, just send it back
```

```
10       return msg;
11     }
12     msg.setResponse(true); // Make message a response
13     // Get candidate ID and vote count
14     int candidate = msg.getCandidateID();
15     Long count = results.get(candidate);
16     if (count == null) {
17       count = 0L; // Candidate does not exist
18     }
19     if (!msg.isInquiry()) {
20       results.put(candidate, ++count); // If vote, increment count
21     }
22     msg.setVoteCount(count);
23     return msg;
24   }
25 }
```

VoteService.java

1. **Create map of candidate ID to vote count:** line 6

   For inquiries, the given candidate ID is used to look up the candidate's vote count in the map. For votes, the incremented vote count is stored back in the map.

2. handleRequest(): lines 8-24

   - **Return a response:** lines 9-12

     If the vote message is already a response, we send it back without processing or modification. Otherwise we set the response flag.

   - **Find current vote count:** lines 13-18

     Find the candidate by ID in the map and fetch the vote count. If the candidate ID does not already exist in the map, set the count to 0.

   - **Update count, if vote:** lines 19-21

     If the candidate did not previously exist, this creates a new mapping; otherwise, it simply modifies an existing mapping.

   - **Set vote count and return message:** lines 22-23

Next we show how to implement a TCP voting client that connects over a TCP socket to the voting server, sends an inquiry followed by a vote, and then receives the inquiry and vote responses.

VoteClientTCP.java

```
0  import java.io.OutputStream;
1  import java.net.Socket;
```

```
2
3  public class VoteClientTCP {
4
5    public static final int CANDIDATEID = 888;
6
7    public static void main(String args[]) throws Exception {
8
9      if (args.length != 2) { // Test for correct # of args
10       throw new IllegalArgumentException("Parameter(s): <Server> <Port>");
11     }
12
13     String destAddr = args[0]; // Destination address
14     int destPort = Integer.parseInt(args[1]); // Destination port
15
16     Socket sock = new Socket(destAddr, destPort);
17     OutputStream out = sock.getOutputStream();
18
19     // Change Bin to Text for a different framing strategy
20     VoteMsgCoder coder = new VoteMsgBinCoder();
21     // Change Length to Delim for a different encoding strategy
22     Framer framer = new LengthFramer(sock.getInputStream());
23
24     // Create an inquiry request (2nd arg = true)
25     VoteMsg msg = new VoteMsg(false, true, CANDIDATEID, 0);
26     byte[] encodedMsg = coder.toWire(msg);
27
28     // Send request
29     System.out.println("Sending Inquiry (" + encodedMsg.length + " bytes): ");
30     System.out.println(msg);
31     framer.frameMsg(encodedMsg, out);
32
33     // Now send a vote
34     msg.setInquiry(false);
35     encodedMsg = coder.toWire(msg);
36     System.out.println("Sending Vote (" + encodedMsg.length + " bytes): ");
37     framer.frameMsg(encodedMsg, out);
38
39     // Receive inquiry response
40     encodedMsg = framer.nextMsg();
41     msg = coder.fromWire(encodedMsg);
42     System.out.println("Received Response (" + encodedMsg.length
43             + " bytes): ");
44     System.out.println(msg);
45
46     // Receive vote response
```

```
47      msg = coder.fromWire(framer.nextMsg());
48      System.out.println("Received Response (" + encodedMsg.length
49              + " bytes): ");
50      System.out.println(msg);
51
52      sock.close();
53    }
54  }
```

VoteClientTCP.java

1. **Process arguments:** lines 9–14

2. **Create socket, get output stream:** lines 16–17

3. **Create binary coder and length-based framer:** lines 20–22
   We will encode/decode our vote messages using a coder. We elect to use a binary encoder for our protocol. Next, since TCP is a stream-based service, we need to provide our own framing. Here we use the LengthFramer, which prefixes each message with a length. Note that we could easily switch to using delimiter-based framing and/or text encoding simply by changing the concrete types of our VoteMsgCoder and Framer to VoteMsgTextCoder and DelimFramer, respectively.

4. **Create and send messages:** lines 24–37
   Create, encode, frame and send an inquiry, followed by a vote message for the same candidate.

5. **Get and parse responses:** lines 39–50
   The nextMsg() method returns the contents of the next encoded message, which we parse/decode via fromWire().

6. **Close socket:** line 52

Next we demonstrate the TCP version of the vote server. Here the server repeatedly accepts a new client connection and uses the VoteService to generate responses to the client vote messages.

VoteServerTCP.java

```
0  import java.io.IOException;
1  import java.net.ServerSocket;
2  import java.net.Socket;
3
4  public class VoteServerTCP {
5
6    public static void main(String args[]) throws Exception {
```

```
7
8     if (args.length != 1) { // Test for correct # of args
9       throw new IllegalArgumentException("Parameter(s): <Port>");
10    }
11
12    int port = Integer.parseInt(args[0]); // Receiving Port
13
14    ServerSocket servSock = new ServerSocket(port);
15    // Change Bin to Text on both client and server for different encoding
16    VoteMsgCoder coder = new VoteMsgBinCoder();
17    VoteService service = new VoteService();
18
19    while (true) {
20      Socket clntSock = servSock.accept();
21      System.out.println("Handling client at " + clntSock.getRemoteSocketAddress());
22      // Change Length to Delim for a different framing strategy
23      Framer framer = new LengthFramer(clntSock.getInputStream());
24      try {
25        byte[] req;
26        while ((req = framer.nextMsg()) != null) {
27          System.out.println("Received message (" + req.length + " bytes)");
28          VoteMsg responseMsg = service.handleRequest(coder.fromWire(req));
29          framer.frameMsg(coder.toWire(responseMsg), clntSock.getOutputStream());
30        }
31      } catch (IOException ioe) {
32        System.err.println("Error handling client: " + ioe.getMessage());
33      } finally {
34        System.out.println("Closing connection");
35        clntSock.close();
36      }
37    }
38  }
39 }
```

VoteServerTCP.java

1. **Establish coder and vote service for server:** lines 15-17
2. **Repeatedly accept and handle client connections:** lines 19-37
   - **Accept new client, print address:** lines 20-21
   - **Create framer for client:** line 23
   - **Fetch and decode messages from client:** lines 26-28
     Repeatedly request next message from framer until it returns null, indicating an end of messages.

■ **Process message, send response:** lines 28–29
  Pass the decoded message to the voting service for handling. Encode, frame, and send the returned response message.

The UDP voting client works very similarly to the TCP version. Note that for UDP we don't need to use a framer because UDP maintains message boundaries for us. For UDP, we use the text encoding for our messages; however, this can be easily changed, as long as client and server agree.

VoteClientUDP.java

```
0   import java.io.IOException;
1   import java.net.DatagramPacket;
2   import java.net.DatagramSocket;
3   import java.net.InetAddress;
4   import java.util.Arrays;
5
6   public class VoteClientUDP {
7
8     public static void main(String args[]) throws IOException {
9
10      if (args.length != 3) { // Test for correct # of args
11        throw new IllegalArgumentException("Parameter(s): <Destination>" +
12                                           " <Port> <Candidate#>");
13      }
14
15      InetAddress destAddr = InetAddress.getByName(args[0]); // Destination addr
16      int destPort = Integer.parseInt(args[1]); // Destination port
17      int candidate = Integer.parseInt(args[2]); // 0 <= candidate <= 1000 req'd
18
19      DatagramSocket sock = new DatagramSocket(); // UDP socket for sending
20      sock.connect(destAddr, destPort);
21
22      // Create a voting message (2nd param false = vote)
23      VoteMsg vote = new VoteMsg(false, false, candidate, 0);
24
25      // Change Text to Bin here for a different coding strategy
26      VoteMsgCoder coder = new VoteMsgTextCoder();
27
28      // Send request
29      byte[] encodedVote = coder.toWire(vote);
30      System.out.println("Sending Text-Encoded Request (" + encodedVote.length
31          + " bytes): ");
32      System.out.println(vote);
33      DatagramPacket message = new DatagramPacket(encodedVote, encodedVote.length);
34      sock.send(message);
```

```
35
36      // Receive response
37      message = new DatagramPacket(new byte[VoteMsgTextCoder.MAX_WIRE_LENGTH],
38          VoteMsgTextCoder.MAX_WIRE_LENGTH);
39      sock.receive(message);
40      encodedVote = Arrays.copyOfRange(message.getData(), 0, message.getLength());
41
42      System.out.println("Received Text-Encoded Response (" + encodedVote.length
43          + " bytes): ");
44      vote = coder.fromWire(encodedVote);
45      System.out.println(vote);
46    }
47 }
```

VoteClientUDP.java

1. **Setup** DatagramSocket **and connect:** lines 10-20
   By calling connect(), we don't have to 1) specify a remote address/port for each datagram we send and 2) test the source of any datagrams we receive.

2. **Create vote and coder:** lines 22-26
   This time we use a text coder; however, we could easily change to a binary coder. Note that we don't need a framer because UDP already preserves message boundaries for us as long as each send contains exactly one vote message.

3. **Send request to the server:** lines 28-34

4. **Receive, decode, and print server response:** lines 36-45
   When creating the DatagramPacket, we need to know the maximum message size to avoid datagram truncation. Of course, when we decode the datagram, we only use the actual bytes from the datagram so we use Arrays.copyOfRange() to copy the subsequence of the datagram backing array.

Finally, here is the UDP voting server, which, again, is very similar to the TCP version.

VoteServerUDP.java

```
0  import java.io.IOException;
1  import java.net.DatagramPacket;
2  import java.net.DatagramSocket;
3  import java.util.Arrays;
4
5  public class VoteServerUDP {
6
7    public static void main(String[] args) throws IOException {
8
9      if (args.length != 1) { // Test for correct # of args
10       throw new IllegalArgumentException("Parameter(s): <Port>");
```

```
11      }
12
13      int port = Integer.parseInt(args[0]); // Receiving Port
14
15      DatagramSocket sock = new DatagramSocket(port); // Receive socket
16
17      byte[] inBuffer = new byte[VoteMsgTextCoder.MAX_WIRE_LENGTH];
18      // Change Bin to Text for a different coding approach
19      VoteMsgCoder coder = new VoteMsgTextCoder();
20      VoteService service = new VoteService();
21
22      while (true) {
23        DatagramPacket packet = new DatagramPacket(inBuffer, inBuffer.length);
24        sock.receive(packet);
25        byte[] encodedMsg = Arrays.copyOfRange(packet.getData(), 0, packet.getLength());
26        System.out.println("Handling request from " + packet.getSocketAddress() + " ("
27            + encodedMsg.length + " bytes)");
28
29        try {
30          VoteMsg msg = coder.fromWire(encodedMsg);
31          msg = service.handleRequest(msg);
32          packet.setData(coder.toWire(msg));
33          System.out.println("Sending response (" + packet.getLength() + " bytes):");
34          System.out.println(msg);
35          sock.send(packet);
36        } catch (IOException ioe) {
37          System.err.println("Parse error in message: " + ioe.getMessage());
38        }
39      }
40    }
41  }
```

VoteServerUDP.java

1. **Setup:** lines 17–20
   Create reception buffer, coder, and vote service for server.

2. **Repeatedly accept and handle client vote messages:** lines 22–39

   - **Set up** DatagramPacket **to receive:** line 23
     Reset the data area to the input buffer on each iteration.

   - **Receive datagram, extract data:** lines 24–25
     UDP does the framing for us!

   - **Decode and handle request:** lines 30–31
     The service returns a response to the message.

   - **Encode and send response message:** lines 32–35

3.6 Wrapping Up

We have seen how primitive types can be represented as sequences of bytes for transmission "on the wire." We have also considered some of the subtleties of encoding text strings, and some basic methods of framing and parsing messages. We saw examples of both text-oriented and binary-encoded protocols.

It is probably worth reiterating something we said in the Preface: this chapter will by no means make you an expert! That takes a great deal of experience. But the code from this chapter can be used as a starting point for further explorations.

3.7 Exercises

1. Positive integers larger than $2^{31} - 1$ (and less than $2^{32} - 1$) cannot be represented as ints in Java, yet they can be represented as 32-bit binary numbers. Write a method to write such an integer to a stream. It should take a long and an OutputStream as parameters.

2. Extend the DelimFramer class to handle arbitrary multiple-byte delimiters. Be sure your implementation is efficient.

3. Extend the DelimFramer to perform "byte stuffing," so messages containing the delimiter can be transmitted. (See any decent networking text for the algorithm.)

4. Assuming that all byte values are equally likely, what is the probability that a message consisting of random bits will pass the "magic test" in VoteMsgBin? Suppose an ASCII-encoded text message is sent to a program expecting a binary-encoded voteMsg. Which characters would enable the message to pass the "magic test" if they are the first in the message?

5. The encodeIntBigEndian() method of BruteForceEncoding only works if several preconditions are met such as $0 \leq size \leq 8$. Modify the method to test for these preconditions and throw an exception if any are violated.

chapter **4**

Beyond the Basics

$\mathbf{T}$he client and server examples in Chapter 2 demonstrate the basic model for programming with sockets in Java. The next step is to apply these concepts in various programming models, such as multitasking, nonblocking I/O, and broadcasting.

4.1 Multitasking

Our basic TCP echo server from Chapter 2 handles one client at a time. If a client connects while another is already being serviced, the server will not echo the new client's data until it has finished with the current client, although the new client will be able to send data as soon as it connects. This type of server is known as an *iterative server*. Iterative servers handle clients sequentially, finishing with one client before servicing the next. They work best for applications where each client requires a small, bounded amount of server connection time; however, if the time to handle a client can be long, the wait experienced by subsequent clients may be unacceptable.

To demonstrate the problem, add a 10-second sleep using Thread.sleep() after the Socket constructor call in TCPEchoClient.java and experiment with several clients simultaneously accessing the TCP echo server. Here the sleep call simulates an operation that takes significant time, such as slow file or network I/O. Note that a new client must wait for all already-connected clients to complete before it gets service.

What we need is some way for each connection to proceed independently, without interfering with other connections. Java *threads* provide exactly that: a convenient mechanism allowing servers to handle many clients simultaneously. Using threads, a single application can work on several tasks concurrently, as if multiple copies of the Java Virtual Machine were running. (In reality, a single copy of the JVM is shared or multiplexed among the different threads.) In our echo server, we can give responsibility for each client to an independently executing thread. All of the examples we have seen so far consist of a single thread, which simply executes the main() method.

In this section we describe two approaches to coding *concurrent servers*, namely, *thread-per-client*, where a new thread is spawned to handle each client connection, and *thread pool*, where connections are assigned to a prespawned set of threads. We shall also describe the built-in Java facilities that simplify the use of these strategies for multithreaded servers.

4.1.1   Java Threads

Java provides two approaches for performing a task in a new thread: 1) defining a subclass of the Thread class with a run() method that performs the task, and instantiating it; or 2) defining a class that implements the Runnable interface with a run() method that performs the task, and passing an instance of that class to the Thread constructor. In either case, the new thread does not begin execution until its start() method is invoked. The first approach can only be used for classes that do not already extend some other class; therefore, we stick with the second approach, which is always applicable. The Runnable interface contains a single method prototype:

```
interface Runnable {
  void run();
}
```

When the start() method of an instance of Thread is invoked, the JVM causes the instance's run() method to be executed in a new thread, concurrently with all others. Meanwhile, the *original* thread returns from its call to start() and continues its execution independently. (Note that directly calling run() does not create a new thread; instead, the run() method is simply executed in the caller's thread, just like any other method call.) The statements of each thread's run() method are interleaved in a nondeterministic fashion, so in general it is not possible to predict precisely the order in which things will happen in different threads.

In the following example, ThreadExample.java implements the Runnable interface with a run() method that repeatedly prints a greeting to the system output stream.

ThreadExample.java

```
0  import java.util.concurrent.TimeUnit;
1
2  public class ThreadExample implements Runnable {
3
4    private String greeting; // Message to print to console
```

```
 5
 6    public ThreadExample(String greeting) {
 7      this.greeting = greeting;
 8    }
 9
10    public void run() {
11      while (true) {
12        System.out.println(Thread.currentThread().getName() + ":  " + greeting);
13        try {
14          // Sleep 0 to 100 milliseconds
15          TimeUnit.MILLISECONDS.sleep(((long) Math.random() * 100));
16        } catch (InterruptedException e) {
17        } // Should not happen
18      }
19    }
20
21    public static void main(String[] args) {
22      new Thread(new ThreadExample("Hello")).start();
23      new Thread(new ThreadExample("Aloha")).start();
24      new Thread(new ThreadExample("Ciao")).start();
25    }
26  }
```

ThreadExample.java

1. **Declaration of implementation of the Runnable interface:** line 2
   Since ThreadExample implements the Runnable interface, it can be passed to the constructor of Thread. If ThreadExample fails to provide a run() method, the compiler will complain.

2. **Member variables and constructor:** lines 4–8
   Each instance of ThreadExample contains its own greeting string.

3. run(): lines 10–19
   Loop forever performing:

   ■ **Print the thread name and instance greeting:** line 12
   The static method Thread.currentThread() returns a reference to the thread from which it is called, and getName() returns a string containing the name of that thread.

   ■ **Suspend thread:** lines 13–17
   After printing its instance's greeting message, each thread sleeps for a random amount of time (between 0 and 100 milliseconds) by calling the static method Thread.sleep(), which takes the number of milliseconds to sleep as a parameter. Math.random() returns a random double between 0.0 and 1.0. Thread.sleep() can be interrupted by another thread, in which case an InterruptedException is thrown. Our example does not include an interrupt call, so the exception will not happen in this application.

4. `main()`: lines 21–25

Each of the three statements in `main()` does the following: 1) creates a new instance of `ThreadExample` with a different greeting string, 2) passes this new instance to the constructor of `Thread`, and 3) calls the new `Thread` instance's `start()` method. Each thread independently executes the `run()` method of `ThreadExample`, while the main thread terminates. Note that the JVM does not terminate until all nondaemon (see `Thread` API) threads terminate.

Upon execution, an interleaving of the three greeting messages is printed to the console. The exact interleaving of the numbers depends upon various factors that in general are not observable. Threads are perfect for implementing servers like our example, in which each client's processing is independent of that provided to every other client. However, it is a different story when client processing involves updating information that is *shared* across threads on the server. In that case, great care must be taken to ensure that different threads are properly *synchronized* with respect to the shared data; otherwise, the shared information can get into an inconsistent state, and moreover, the problem can be very difficult to trace. A full treatment of techniques and facilities for concurrency would require a book of its own. The book by Goetz et al. [9], for example, is excellent.

4.1.2   Server Protocol

Since the multitasking server approaches we are going to describe are independent of the particular client-server protocol, we want to be able to use the same protocol implementation for both. The code for the echo protocol is given in the class `EchoProtocol`. This class encapsulates the per-client processing in the static method `handleEchoClient()`. This code is almost identical to the connection-handling portion of `TCPEchoServer.java`, except that a logging capability (described shortly) has been added; the method takes references to the client `Socket` and the `Logger` instance as arguments.

The class implements `Runnable` (the `run()` method simply invokes `handle EchoClient()` with the instance's `Socket` and `Logger` references), so we can create a thread that independently executes `run()`. Alternatively, the server-side protocol processing can be invoked by calling the static method directly (passing it the `Socket` and `Logger` references).

EchoProtocol.java

```
0  import java.io.IOException;
1  import java.io.InputStream;
2  import java.io.OutputStream;
3  import java.net.Socket;
4  import java.util.logging.Level;
5  import java.util.logging.Logger;
6
7  public class EchoProtocol implements Runnable {
8    private static final int BUFSIZE = 32; // Size (in bytes) of I/O buffer
```

```
 9    private Socket clntSock;                // Socket connect to client
10    private Logger logger;                  // Server logger
11
12    public EchoProtocol(Socket clntSock, Logger logger) {
13      this.clntSock = clntSock;
14      this.logger = logger;
15    }
16
17    public static void handleEchoClient(Socket clntSock, Logger logger) {
18      try {
19        // Get the input and output I/O streams from socket
20        InputStream in = clntSock.getInputStream();
21        OutputStream out = clntSock.getOutputStream();
22
23        int recvMsgSize; // Size of received message
24        int totalBytesEchoed = 0; // Bytes received from client
25        byte[] echoBuffer = new byte[BUFSIZE]; // Receive Buffer
26        // Receive until client closes connection, indicated by -1
27        while ((recvMsgSize = in.read(echoBuffer)) != -1) {
28          out.write(echoBuffer, 0, recvMsgSize);
29          totalBytesEchoed += recvMsgSize;
30        }
31
32        logger.info("Client " + clntSock.getRemoteSocketAddress() + ", echoed "
33            + totalBytesEchoed + " bytes.");
34
35      } catch (IOException ex) {
36        logger.log(Level.WARNING, "Exception in echo protocol", ex);
37      } finally {
38        try {
39          clntSock.close();
40        } catch (IOException e) {
41        }
42      }
43    }
44
45    public void run() {
46      handleEchoClient(clntSock, logger);
47    }
48  }
```

EchoProtocol.java

1. **Declaration of implementation of the Runnable interface:** line 7

2. **Member variables and constructor:** lines 8–15

Each instance of `EchoProtocol` contains a socket for the connection and a reference to the logger instance.

3. `handleEchoClient()`: lines 17–43

Implement the echo protocol:

- **Get the input/output streams from the socket:** lines 20–21

- **Receive and echo:** lines 25–30
  Loop until the connection is closed (as indicated by `read()` returning −1), writing whatever is received back immediately.

- **Record the connection details in the log:** lines 32–33
  Record the `SocketAddress` of the remote end along with the number of bytes echoed.

- **Handle exceptions:** line 36
  Log any exceptions.

Your server is up and running with thousands of clients per minute. Now a user reports a problem. How do you determine what happened? Is the problem at your server? Perhaps the client is violating the protocol. To deal with this scenario, most servers log their activities. This practice is so common that Java now includes built-in logging facilities in the `java.util.logging` package. We provide a very basic introduction to logging here; however, be aware that there are many more features to enterprise-level logging.

We begin with the `Logger` class, which represents a logging facility that may be local or remote. Through an instance of this class, we can record the various server activities as shown in `EchoProtocol`. You may use several loggers in your server, each serving a different purpose and potentially behaving in a different way. For example, you may have separate loggers for operations, security, and error messages. In Java each logger is identified by a globally unique name. To get an instance of `Logger`, call the static factory method `Logger.getLogger()` as follows:

```
Logger logger = Logger.getLogger("practical");
```

This fetches the logger named "practical". If a logger by that name does not exist, a new logger is created; otherwise, the existing logger instance is returned. No matter how many times you get the "practical" logger in your program, the same instance is returned.

Now that you have logging, what should you log? Well, it depends on what you are doing. If the server is operating normally, you may not want to log every single step the server takes because logging consumes resources such as space for storing log entries and server processor time for writing each entry. On the other hand, if you are trying to debug, you may want to log each and every step. To deal with this, logging typically includes the notion of the *level*, or severity, of log entries. The `Level` class encapsulates the notion of the importance of messages. Each instance of `Logger` has a current level, and each message logged has an associated level; messages with levels below the instance's current level are discarded (i.e., not logged). Each level has an associated integer *value*, so that levels are comparable and can be ordered. Seven system-recognized instances of `Level` are defined; other, user-specific, levels can be created, but there is rarely any need to do so. The built-in levels (defined as static fields of the class `Level`) are: SEVERE, WARNING, INFO, CONFIG, FINE, FINER, and FINEST.

So when you log, where do the messages go? The logger sends messages to one or more Handlers, which "handle" publishing the messages. By default, a logger has a single ConsoleHandler that prints messages to System.err. You can change the handler or add additional handlers to a logger (e.g., FileHandler). Note that like a logger, a handler has a minimum log level, so for a message to be published its level must be above *both* the logger and handlers' threshold. Loggers and handlers are highly configurable, including their minimum level.

An important characteristic of Logger for our purposes is that it is *thread-safe*—that is, its methods can be called from different threads running concurrently without requiring additional synchronization among the callers. Without this feature, different messages logged by different threads might end up being interleaved in the log!

Logger: Finding/Creating

```
static Logger getLogger(String name)
static Logger getLogger(String name, String resourceBundleName)
```

The static factory methods return the named Logger, creating it if necessary.

Once we have the logger, we need to ... well ... log. Logger provides fine-grained logging facilities that differentiate between the level and even context (method call, exception, etc.) of the message.

Logger: Logging a message

```
void severe(String msg)
void warning(String msg)
void info(String msg)
void config(String msg)
void fine(String msg)
void finer(String msg)
void finest(String msg)

void entering(String sourceClass, String sourceMethod)
void entering(String sourceClass, String sourceMethod, Object param)
void entering(String sourceClass, String sourceMethod, Object[] params)
void exiting(String sourceClass, String sourceMethod)
void exiting(String sourceClass, String sourceMethod, Object result)
void throwing(String sourceClass, String sourceMethod, Throwable thrown)

void log(Level level, String msg)
void log(Level level, String msg, Throwable thrown)
```

The severe(), warning(), etc. methods log the given message at the level specified by the method name. The entering() and exiting() methods log entering and exiting the given method from the given class. Note that you may optionally specify additional information such as parameters and return values. The throwing() method logs an exception thrown in a specific method. The log() methods provide a generic logging method where level, message, and (optionally) exception can be logged. Note that many other logging methods exist; we are only noting the major types here.

We may want to customize our logger by setting the minimum logging level or the handlers for logging messages.

Logger: Setting/Getting the level and handlers

```
Handler[] getHandlers()
void addHandler(Handler handler)
void removeHandler(Handler handler)

Level getLevel()
void setLevel(Level newLevel)
boolean isLoggable(Level level)
```

The getHandlers() method returns an array of all handlers associated with the logger. The addHandler() and removeHandler() methods allow addition/removal of handlers to/from the logger. The getLevel() and setLevel() methods get/set the minimum logging level. The isLoggable() method returns true if the given level will be logged by the logger.

We are now ready to introduce some different approaches to concurrent servers.

4.1.3 Thread-per-Client

In a *thread-per-client* server, a new thread is created to handle each connection. The server executes a loop that runs forever, listening for connections on a specified port and repeatedly accepting an incoming connection from a client and then spawning a new thread to handle that connection.

TCPEchoServerThread.java implements the thread-per-client architecture. It is very similar to the iterative server, using a single loop to receive and process client requests. The main difference is that it creates a thread to handle the connection instead of handling it directly. (This is possible because EchoProtocol implements the Runnable interface.) Thus, when several clients connect at approximately the same time, later ones do not have to wait for the server to finish with the earlier ones before they get service. Instead, they all appear to receive service (albeit at a somewhat slower rate) at the same time.

TCPEchoServerThread.java

```
0   import java.io.IOException;
1   import java.net.ServerSocket;
2   import java.net.Socket;
3   import java.util.logging.Logger;
4
5   public class TCPEchoServerThread {
6
7     public static void main(String[] args) throws IOException {
8
9       if (args.length != 1) { // Test for correct # of args
10        throw new IllegalArgumentException("Parameter(s): <Port>");
11      }
12
13      int echoServPort = Integer.parseInt(args[0]); // Server port
14
15      // Create a server socket to accept client connection requests
16      ServerSocket servSock = new ServerSocket(echoServPort);
17
18      Logger logger = Logger.getLogger("practical");
19
20      // Run forever, accepting and spawning a thread for each connection
21      while (true) {
22        Socket clntSock = servSock.accept(); // Block waiting for connection
23        // Spawn thread to handle new connection
24        Thread thread = new Thread(new EchoProtocol(clntSock, logger));
25        thread.start();
26        logger.info("Created and started Thread " + thread.getName());
27      }
28      /* NOT REACHED */
29    }
30  }
```

TCPEchoServerThread.java

1. **Parameter parsing and server socket/logger creation:** lines 9–18
2. **Loop forever, handling incoming connections:** lines 21–27
   - **Accept an incoming connection:** line 22
   - **Create a new instance of** Thread **to handle the new connection:** line 24

Since EchoProtocol implements the Runnable interface, we can give our new instance to the Thread constructor, and the new thread will execute the run() method of EchoProtocol (which calls handleEchoClient()) when start() is invoked.

▪ **Start the new thread for the connection and log it:** lines 25–26
The getName() method of Thread returns a String containing a name for the new thread.

4.1.4   Thread Pool

Every new thread consumes system resources: spawning a thread takes CPU cycles and each thread has its own data structures (e.g., stacks) that consume system memory. In addition, when one thread *blocks*, the JVM saves its state, selects another thread to run, and restores the state of the chosen thread in what is called a *context switch*. As the number of threads increases, more and more system resources are consumed by thread overhead. Eventually, the system is spending more time dealing with context switching and thread management than with servicing connections. At that point, adding an additional thread may actually *increase* client service time.

We can avoid this problem by limiting the total number of threads and reusing threads. Instead of spawning a new thread for each connection, the server creates a *thread pool* on start-up by spawning a fixed number of threads. When a new client connection arrives at the server, it is assigned to a thread from the pool. When the thread finishes with the client, it returns to the pool, ready to handle another request. Connection requests that arrive when all threads in the pool are busy are queued to be serviced by the next available thread.

Like the thread-per-client server, a thread-pool server begins by creating a ServerSocket. Then it spawns *N* threads, each of which loops forever, accepting connections from the (shared) ServerSocket instance. When multiple threads simultaneously call accept() on the same Server-Socket instance, they all block until a connection is established. Then the system selects one thread, and the Socket instance for the new connection is returned *only in that thread*. The other threads remain blocked until the next connection is established and another lucky winner is chosen.

Since each thread in the pool loops forever, processing connections one by one, a thread-pool server is really like a set of iterative servers. Unlike the thread-per-client server, a thread-pool thread does not terminate when it finishes with a client. Instead, it starts over again, blocking on accept(). An example of the thread-pool paradigm is shown in TCPEchoServerPool.java.

TCPEchoServerPool.java

```
0   import java.io.IOException;
1   import java.net.ServerSocket;
2   import java.net.Socket;
3   import java.util.logging.Level;
4   import java.util.logging.Logger;
5
```

```
6  public class TCPEchoServerPool {
7
8    public static void main(String[] args) throws IOException {
9
10     if (args.length != 2) { // Test for correct # of args
11       throw new IllegalArgumentException("Parameter(s): <Port> <Threads>");
12     }
13
14     int echoServPort = Integer.parseInt(args[0]); // Server port
15     int threadPoolSize = Integer.parseInt(args[1]);
16
17     // Create a server socket to accept client connection requests
18     final ServerSocket servSock = new ServerSocket(echoServPort);
19
20     final Logger logger = Logger.getLogger("practical");
21
22     // Spawn a fixed number of threads to service clients
23     for (int i = 0; i < threadPoolSize; i++) {
24       Thread thread = new Thread() {
25         public void run() {
26           while (true) {
27             try {
28               Socket clntSock = servSock.accept(); // Wait for a connection
29               EchoProtocol.handleEchoClient(clntSock, logger); // Handle it
30             } catch (IOException ex) {
31               logger.log(Level.WARNING, "Client accept failed", ex);
32             }
33           }
34         }
35       };
36       thread.start();
37       logger.info("Created and started Thread = " + thread.getName());
38     }
39   }
40 }
```

TCPEchoServerPool.java

1. **Setup:** lines 10–20
   The port number to listen on and the number of threads are both passed as arguments to main(). After parsing them we create the ServerSocket and Logger instances. Note that both have to be declared final, because they are referenced inside the anonymous class instance created below.

2. **Create and start _threadPoolSize_ new threads:** lines 23–38
   For each loop iteration, an instance of an anonymous class that extends Thread is created. When the start() method of this instance is called, the thread executes the run() method

of this anonymous class. The `run()` method loops forever, accepting a connection and then giving it to EchoProtocol for service.

∎ **Accept an incoming connection:** line 28
Since there are N different threads executing the same loop, up to N threads can be blocked on *servSock*'s `accept()`, waiting for an incoming connection. The system ensures that only one thread gets a Socket for any particular connection. If no threads are blocked on `accept()` when a client connection is established (that is, if they are all busy servicing other connections), the new connection is queued by the system until the next call to `accept()` (see Section 6.4.1).

∎ **Pass the client socket to** `EchoProtocol.handleEchoClient`: line 29
The `handleEchoClient()` method encapsulates knowledge of the protocol details. It logs the connection when it finishes, as well as any exceptions encountered along the way.

∎ **Handle exception from** `accept()`: line 31

Since threads are reused, the thread-pool solution only pays the overhead of thread creation N times, irrespective of the total number of client connections. Since we control the maximum number of simultaneously executing threads, we can control scheduling and resource overhead. Of course, if we spawn too few threads, we can still have clients waiting a long time for service; therefore, the size of the thread pool needs to be tuned to the load, so that client connection time is minimized. The ideal would be a dispatching facility that expands the thread pool (up to a limit) when the load increases, and shrinks it to minimize overhead during times when the load is light. It turns out that Java has just such a facility; we describe it in the next section.

4.1.5   System-Managed Dispatching: The Executor Interface

In the previous subsections, we have seen that encapsulating the details of the client-server protocol (as in `EchoProtocol.java`) lets us use different "dispatching" methods with the same protocol implementation (e.g., `TCPEchoServerThread.java` and `TCPEchoServerThreadPool.java`). In fact the same thing is true for the dispatching methods themselves. The interface Executor (part of the `java.util.concurrent` package) represents an object that executes Runnable instances according to some strategy, which may include details about queueing and scheduling, or how jobs are selected for execution. The Executor interface specifies a single method:

```
interface Executor {
  void execute(Runnable task);
}
```

Java provides a number of built-in implementations of Executor that are convenient and simple to use, and others that are extensively configurable. Some of these offer handling for messy details like thread maintenance. For example, if a thread stops because of an uncaught exception or other failure, they automatically spawn a new thread to replace it.

The ExecutorService interface extends Executor to provide a more sophisticated facility that allows a service to be shut down, either gracefully or abruptly. ExecutorService also allows for tasks to return a result, through the Callable interface, which is like Runnable, only with a return value.

Instances of ExecutorService can be obtained by calling various static factory methods of the convenience class Executors. The program TCPEchoServerExecutor.java illustrates the use of the basic Executor facilities.

TCPEchoServerExecutor.java

```
0   import java.io.IOException;
1   import java.net.ServerSocket;
2   import java.net.Socket;
3   import java.util.concurrent.Executor;
4   import java.util.concurrent.Executors;
5   import java.util.logging.Logger;
6
7   public class TCPEchoServerExecutor {
8
9     public static void main(String[] args) throws IOException {
10
11      if (args.length != 1) { // Test for correct # of args
12        throw new IllegalArgumentException("Parameter(s): <Port>");
13      }
14
15      int echoServPort = Integer.parseInt(args[0]); // Server port
16
17      // Create a server socket to accept client connection requests
18      ServerSocket servSock = new ServerSocket(echoServPort);
19
20      Logger logger = Logger.getLogger("practical");
21
22      Executor service = Executors.newCachedThreadPool();  // Dispatch svc
23
24      // Run forever, accepting and spawning a thread for each connection
25      while (true) {
26        Socket clntSock = servSock.accept(); // Block waiting for connection
27        service.execute(new EchoProtocol(clntSock, logger));
28      }
29      /* NOT REACHED */
30    }
31  }
```

1. **Setup:** lines 11-20
   The port is the only argument. We create the ServerSocket and Logger instances as before; they need not be declared final here, because we do not need an anonymous Thread subclass.

2. **Get an** Executor: line 22
   The static factory method newCachedThreadPool() of class Executors creates an instance of ExecutorService. When its execute() method is invoked with a Runnable instance, the executor service creates a new thread to handle the task if necessary. However, it first tries to reuse an existing thread. When a thread has been idle for at least 60 seconds, it is removed from the pool. This is almost always going to be more efficient than either of the last two TCPEchoServer* examples.

3. **Loop forever, accepting connections and executing them:** lines 25-28
   When a new connection arrives, a new EchoProtocol instance is created and passed to the execute() method of *service*, which either hands it off to an already-existing thread or creates a new thread to handle it. Note that in the steady state, the cached thread pool Executor service ends up having about the right number of threads, so that each thread stays busy and creation/destruction of threads is rare.

Once we have a server designed to use Executor for dispatching clients, we can change dispatching strategies simply by changing the kind of Executor we instantiate. For example, if we wanted to use a fixed-size thread pool as in our TCPEchoServerPool.java example, it is a matter of changing one line associated with setting the dispatch service:

```
Executor service = Executors.newFixedThreadPool(threadPoolSize);
```

We could switch to a single thread to execute all connections either by specifying a pool size of 1, or by the following call:

```
Executor service = Executors.newSingleThreadExecutor();
```

In the Executor approach, if the single "worker" thread dies because of some failure, the Executor will replace it with a new thread. Also, tasks are queued inside the Executor, instead of being queued inside the networking system, as they were in our original server. Note that we've only scratched the surface of Java's concurrency package.

4.2 Blocking and Timeouts

Socket I/O calls may block for several reasons. Data input methods read() and receive() block if data is not available. A write() on a TCP socket may block if there is not sufficient space to buffer the transmitted data. The accept() method of ServerSocket() and the Socket constructor both block until a connection has been established (see Section 6.4). Meanwhile, long round-trip times, high error rate connections, and slow (or deceased) servers may cause connection establishment to take a long time. In all of these cases, the method returns only after the request has been satisfied. Of course, a blocked method call halts progress of the application (and makes the thread that is running it useless).

What about a program that has other tasks to perform while waiting for call completion (e.g., updating the "busy" cursor or responding to user requests)? These programs may have no time to wait on a blocked method call. What about lost UDP datagrams? If we block waiting to receive a datagram and it is lost, we could block indefinitely. Here we explore the various blocking methods and approaches for limiting blocking behavior. In Chapter 5 we'll encounter the more powerful nonblocking facilities available through the NIO package.

4.2.1 accept(), read(), and receive()

For these methods, we can set a bound on the maximum time (in milliseconds) to block, using the setSoTimeout() method of Socket, ServerSocket, and DatagramSocket. If the specified time elapses before the method returns, an InterruptedIOException is thrown. For Socket instances, we can also use the available() method of the socket's InputStream to check for available data before calling read().

4.2.2 Connecting and Writing

The Socket constructor attempts to establish a connection to the host and port supplied as arguments, blocking until either the connection is established or a system-imposed timeout occurs. Unfortunately, the system-imposed timeout is long, and Java does not provide any means of shortening it. To fix this, call the parameterless constructor for Socket, which returns an unconnected instance. To establish a connection, call the connect() method on the newly constructed socket and specify both a remote endpoint and timeout (milliseconds).

A write() call blocks until the last byte written is copied into the TCP implementation's local buffer; if the available buffer space is smaller than the size of the write, some data must be successfully transferred to the other end of the connection before the call to write() will return (see Section 6.1 for details). Thus, the amount of time that a write() may block is ultimately controlled by the receiving application. Unfortunately, Java currently does not provide any way to cause a write() to time out, nor can it be interrupted by another thread. Therefore, any protocol that sends a large enough amount of data over a Socket instance can block for an unbounded amount of time. (See Section 6.2 for a discussion of the potentially disastrous consequences of this.)

4.2.3 Limiting Per-Client Time

Suppose we want to implement the Echo protocol with a limit on the amount of time taken to service each client. That is, we define a target, TIMELIMIT, and implement the protocol in such a way that after TIMELIMIT milliseconds, the protocol instance is terminated. The protocol instance keeps track of the amount of time remaining, and uses setSoTimeout() to ensure that no read() call blocks for longer than that time. Since there is no way to bound the duration of a write() call, we cannot really guarantee that the time limit will hold. Nevertheless, Time-limitEchoProtocol.java implements this approach; to use it with TCPEchoServerExecutor.java, simply change the second line of the body of the while loop to:

```
service.execute(new TimeLimitEchoProtocol(clntSock, logger));
```

Again, Chapter 5 will cover more powerful mechanisms that can limit the time that threads can block—on all I/O calls, including writes—using the facilities of the NIO package.

TimeLimitEchoProtocol.java

```
0   import java.io.IOException;
1   import java.io.InputStream;
2   import java.io.OutputStream;
3   import java.net.Socket;
4   import java.util.logging.Level;
5   import java.util.logging.Logger;
6
7   class TimelimitEchoProtocol implements Runnable {
8     private static final int BUFSIZE = 32;  // Size (bytes) of buffer
9     private static final String TIMELIMIT = "10000";  // Default limit (ms)
10    private static final String TIMELIMITPROP = "Timelimit";  // Property
11
12    private static int timelimit;
13    private Socket clntSock;
14    private Logger logger;
15
16    public TimelimitEchoProtocol(Socket clntSock, Logger logger) {
17      this.clntSock = clntSock;
18      this.logger = logger;
19      // Get the time limit from the System properties or take the default
20      timelimit = Integer.parseInt(System.getProperty(TIMELIMITPROP,TIMELIMIT));
21    }
22
23    public static void handleEchoClient(Socket clntSock, Logger logger) {
24
25      try {
26        // Get the input and output I/O streams from socket
27        InputStream in = clntSock.getInputStream();
28        OutputStream out = clntSock.getOutputStream();
29        int recvMsgSize;                       // Size of received message
30        int totalBytesEchoed = 0;              // Bytes received from client
31        byte[] echoBuffer = new byte[BUFSIZE];  // Receive buffer
32        long endTime = System.currentTimeMillis() + timelimit;
33        int timeBoundMillis = timelimit;
```

```
34
35      clntSock.setSoTimeout(timeBoundMillis);
36      // Receive until client closes connection, indicated by -1
37      while ((timeBoundMillis > 0) &&      // catch zero values
38             ((recvMsgSize = in.read(echoBuffer)) != -1)) {
39        out.write(echoBuffer, 0, recvMsgSize);
40        totalBytesEchoed += recvMsgSize;
41        timeBoundMillis = (int) (endTime - System.currentTimeMillis()) ;
42        clntSock.setSoTimeout(timeBoundMillis);
43      }
44      logger.info("Client " + clntSock.getRemoteSocketAddress() +
45               ", echoed " + totalBytesEchoed + " bytes.");
46    } catch (IOException ex) {
47      logger.log(Level.WARNING, "Exception in echo protocol", ex);
48    }
49  }
50
51  public void run() {
52    handleEchoClient(this.clntSock, this.logger);
53  }
54 }
```

TimeLimitEchoProtocol.java

The `TimelimitEchoProtocol` class is similar to the `EchoProtocol` class, except that it attempts to bound the total time an echo connection can exist to 10 seconds. At the time the `handleEchoClient()` method is invoked, a deadline is computed using the current time and the time bound. After each `read()`, the time between the current time and the deadline is computed, and the socket timeout is set to the remaining time.

4.3 Multiple Recipients

So far all of our sockets have dealt with communication between exactly two entities, usually a server and a client. Such one-to-one communication is sometimes called *unicast*. Some information is of interest to multiple recipients. In such cases, we could unicast a copy of the data to each recipient, but this may be very inefficient. Unicasting multiple copies over a single network connection wastes bandwidth by sending the same information multiple times. In fact, if we want to send data at a fixed rate, the bandwidth of our network connection defines a hard limit on the number of receivers we can support. For example, if our video server sends 1Mbps streams and its network connection is only 3Mbps (a healthy connection rate), we can only support three simultaneous users.

Fortunately, networks provide a way to use bandwidth more efficiently. Instead of making the sender responsible for duplicating packets, we can give this job to the network. In our video server example, we send a single copy of the stream across the server's connection to the network, which then duplicates the data only when appropriate. With this model of duplication, the server uses only 1Mbps across its connection to the network, irrespective of the number of clients.

There are two types of one-to-many service: *broadcast* and *multicast.* With broadcast, all hosts on the (local) network receive a copy of the message. With multicast, the message is sent to a *multicast address,* and the network delivers it only to those hosts that have indicated that they want to receive messages sent to that address. In general, only UDP sockets are allowed to broadcast or multicast.

4.3.1   Broadcast

Broadcasting UDP datagrams is similar to unicasting datagrams, except that a *broadcast address* is used instead of a regular (unicast) IP address. Note that IPv6 does not explicitly provide broadcast addresses; however, there is a special all-nodes, link-local-scope multicast address, FFO2::1, that multicasts to all nodes on a link. The IPv4 *local broadcast* address (255.255.255.255) sends the message to every host on the same broadcast network. Local broadcast messages are never forwarded by routers. A host on an Ethernet network can send a message to all other hosts on that same Ethernet, but the message will not be forwarded by a router. IPv4 also specifies *directed broadcast* addresses, which allow broadcasts to all hosts on a specified network; however, since most Internet routers do not forward directed broadcasts, we do not deal with them here.

There is no networkwide broadcast address that can be used to send a message to all hosts. To see why, consider the impact of a broadcast to every host on the Internet. Sending a single datagram would result in a very, very large number of packet duplications by the routers, and bandwidth would be consumed on each and every network. The consequences of misuse (malicious or accidental) are too great, so the designers of IP left such an Internetwide broadcast facility out on purpose.

Even so, local broadcast can be very useful. Often, it is used in state exchange for network games where the players are all on the same local (broadcast) network. In Java, the code for unicasting and broadcasting is the same. To play with broadcasting applications, we can simply use our VoteClientUDP.java with a broadcast destination address. There is one problem. Can you find it? *Hint:* You cannot use connect with broadcast. Run VoteServerUDP.java as you did before (except that you can run several receivers at one time). *Caveat:* Some operating systems do not give regular users permission to broadcast, in which case this will not work.

4.3.2   Multicast

As with broadcast, one of the main differences between multicast and unicast is the form of the address. A multicast address identifies a set of receivers. The designers of IP allocated a range of the address space dedicated to multicast, specifically 224.0.0.0 to 239.255.255.255 for IPv4 and any address starting with FF for IPv6. With the exception of a few reserved multicast addresses, a sender can send datagrams addressed to any address in this range. In Java, multicast applications generally communicate using an instance of MulticastSocket, a subclass of DatagramSocket. It is important to understand that a MulticastSocket is actually a UDP socket (DatagramSocket), with some extra multicast-specific attributes that can be controlled. Our next examples implement a multicast sender and receiver of vote messages.

VoteMulticastSender.java

```
0   import java.io.IOException;
1   import java.net.DatagramPacket;
2   import java.net.InetAddress;
3   import java.net.MulticastSocket;
4
5   public class VoteMulticastSender {
6
7     public static final int CANDIDATEID = 475;
8
9     public static void main(String args[]) throws IOException {
10
11      if ((args.length < 2) || (args.length > 3)) { // Test # of args
12        throw new IllegalArgumentException("Parameter(s): <Multicast Addr> <Port> [<TTL>]");
13      }
14
15      InetAddress destAddr = InetAddress.getByName(args[0]); // Destination
16      if (!destAddr.isMulticastAddress()) { // Test if multicast address
17        throw new IllegalArgumentException("Not a multicast address");
18      }
19
20      int destPort = Integer.parseInt(args[1]); // Destination port
21      int TTL = (args.length == 3) ? Integer.parseInt(args[2]) : 1; // Set TTL
22
23      MulticastSocket sock = new MulticastSocket();
24      sock.setTimeToLive(TTL); // Set TTL for all datagrams
25
26      VoteMsgCoder coder = new VoteMsgTextCoder();
27
28      VoteMsg vote = new VoteMsg(true, true, CANDIDATEID, 1000001L);
29
30      // Create and send a datagram
31      byte[] msg = coder.toWire(vote);
32      DatagramPacket message = new DatagramPacket(msg, msg.length, destAddr, destPort);
33      System.out.println("Sending Text-Encoded Request (" + msg.length + " bytes): ");
```

```
34      System.out.println(vote);
35      sock.send(message);
36
37      sock.close();
38    }
39 }
```

The only significant differences between our unicast and multicast senders are that 1) we verify that the given address is multicast, and 2) we set the initial Time To Live (TTL) value for the multicast datagram. Every IP datagram contains a TTL, initialized to some default value and decremented (usually by one) by each router that forwards the packet. When the TTL reaches zero, the packet is discarded. By setting the initial value of the TTL, we limit the distance a packet can travel from the sender.[1]

Unlike broadcast, network multicast duplicates the message only to a specific set of receivers. This set of receivers, called a *multicast group*, is identified by a shared multicast (or group) address. Receivers need some mechanism to notify the network of their interest in receiving data sent to a particular multicast address, so that the network can forward packets to them. This notification, called *joining a group*, is accomplished with the joinGroup() method of MulticastSocket. Our multicast receiver joins a specified group, receives and prints a single multicast message from that group, and exits.

VoteMulticastReceiver.java

```
0  import java.io.IOException;
1  import java.net.DatagramPacket;
2  import java.net.InetAddress;
3  import java.net.MulticastSocket;
4  import java.util.Arrays;
5
6  public class VoteMulticastReceiver {
7
8    public static void main(String[] args) throws IOException {
9
10      if (args.length != 2) { // Test for correct # of args
11        throw new IllegalArgumentException("Parameter(s): <Multicast Addr> <Port>");
12      }
13
14      InetAddress address = InetAddress.getByName(args[0]); // Multicast address
```

---

[1]The rules for multicast TTL are actually not quite so simple. It is not necessarily the case that a packet with TTL = 4 can travel four hops from the sender; however, it will not travel *more* than four hops.

```
15        if (!address.isMulticastAddress()) { // Test if multicast address
16          throw new IllegalArgumentException("Not a multicast address");
17        }
18
19        int port = Integer.parseInt(args[1]); // Multicast port
20        MulticastSocket sock = new MulticastSocket(port); // for receiving
21        sock.joinGroup(address); // Join the multicast group
22
23        VoteMsgTextCoder coder = new VoteMsgTextCoder();
24
25        // Receive a datagram
26        DatagramPacket packet = new DatagramPacket(new byte[VoteMsgTextCoder.MAX_WIRE_LENGTH],
27            VoteMsgTextCoder.MAX_WIRE_LENGTH);
28        sock.receive(packet);
29
30        VoteMsg vote = coder.fromWire(Arrays.copyOfRange(packet.getData(), 0, packet
31            .getLength()));
32
33        System.out.println("Received Text-Encoded Request (" + packet.getLength()
34            + " bytes): ");
35        System.out.println(vote);
36
37        sock.close();
38    }
39 }
```

VoteMulticastReceiver.java

The only significant difference between our multicast and unicast receiver is that the multicast receiver must join the multicast group by supplying the desired multicast address. The book's Web site also contains another example of a sender and receiver multicast pair. MulticastImageSender.java transmits a set of images (JPEG or GIF) specified on the command line, in three-second intervals. MulticastImageReceiver.java receives each image and displays it in a window.

Multicast datagrams can, in fact, be sent from a DatagramSocket by simply using a multicast address. However, a MulticastSocket has a few capabilities that a DatagramSocket does not, including 1) allowing specification of the datagram TTL, and 2) allowing the interface through which datagrams are sent to the group to be specified/changed (an interface is identified by its Internet address). A multicast receiver, on the other hand, *must* use a MulticastSocket because it needs the ability to join a group.

MulticastSocket is a subclass of DatagramSocket, so it provides all of the DatagramSocket methods. We only present methods specific to or adapted for MulticastSocket.

┌─ **MulticastSocket: Creation** ──┐

```
MulticastSocket()
MulticastSocket(int localPort)
MulticastSocket(SocketAddress bindaddr)
```

These constructors create a multicast-capable UDP socket. If the local port is not specified, or is specified as 0, the socket is bound to any available local port. If the address is specified, the socket is restricted to receiving only on that address.

└──┘

If we wish to receive any datagrams, we need to join a multicast group.

┌─ **MulticastSocket: Group management** ────────────────────────────────────┐

```
void joinGroup(InetAddress groupAddress)
void joinGroup(SocketAddress mcastaddr, NetworkInterface netIf)
void leaveGroup(InetAddress groupAddress)
void leaveGroup(SocketAddress mcastaddr, NetworkInterface netIf)
```

The joinGroup() and leaveGroup() methods manage multicast group membership. A socket may be a member of multiple groups simultaneously. Joining a group of which this socket is already a member or leaving a group of which this socket is not a member may generate an exception. Optionally, you may specify an interface on which to join/leave.

└──┘

┌─ **MulticastSocket: Setting/Getting multicast options** ───────────────────┐

```
int getTimeToLive()
void setTimeToLive(int ttl)
boolean getLoopbackMode()
void setLoopbackMode(boolean disable)
InetAddress getInterface()
NetworkInterface getNetworkInterface()
void setInterface(InetAddress inf)
void setNetworkInterface(NetworkInterface netIf)
```

The getTimeToLive() and setTimeToLive() methods get and set the time-to-live for all datagrams sent on this socket. A socket with loopback mode enabled will receive the datagrams it sends. The getLoopbackMode() and setLoopbackMode() methods set the loopback mode for the multicast socket where setting the loopback mode to TRUE disables loopback. The getInterface(), setInterface(), getNetworkInterface(), setNetworkInterface() methods set the outgoing interface used in sending multicast packets. This is primarily used on hosts with multiple interfaces. The default multicast interface is platform dependent.

The decision to use broadcast or multicast depends on several factors, including the network location of receivers and the knowledge of the communicating parties. The scope of a broadcast on the Internet is restricted to a local broadcast network, placing severe restrictions on the location of the broadcast receivers. Multicast communication may include receivers anywhere in the network,[2] so multicast has the advantage that it can cover a distributed set of receivers. The disadvantage of IP multicast is that receivers must know the address of a multicast group to join. Knowledge of an address is not required to receive broadcast. In some contexts, this makes broadcast a better mechanism than multicast for discovery. All hosts can receive broadcast by default, so it is simple to ask all hosts on a single network a question like "Where's the printer?"

UDP unicast, multicast, and broadcast are all implemented using an underlying UDP socket. The semantics of most implementations are such that a UDP datagram will be delivered to all sockets bound to the destination port of the packet. That is, a DatagramSocket or MulticastSocket instance bound to a local port X (with local address not specified, i.e., a wild card), on a host with address Y will receive any UDP datagram destined for port X that is 1) unicast with destination address Y, 2) multicast to a group that *any* application on Y has joined, or 3) broadcast where it can reach host Y. A receiver can use connect() to limit the datagram source address and port. Also, a DatagramSocket can specify the local unicast address, which prevents delivery of multicast and broadcast packets. See UDPEchoClientTimeout.java for an example of destination address verification and Section 6.5 for details on datagram demultiplexing.

4.4 Controlling Default Behaviors

The TCP/IP protocol developers spent a good deal of time thinking about the default behaviors that would satisfy most applications. (If you doubt this, read RFCs 1122 and 1123, which describe in excruciating detail the recommended behaviors—based on years of experience—for implementations of the TCP/IP protocols.) For most applications, the designers did a good job; however, it is seldom the case that "one size fits all" really fits all. We have already seen an example in our UDP echo client. By default, the receive() method of DatagramSocket blocks indefinitely waiting on a datagram. In our example, we change that behavior by

---

[2]At the time of writing of this book, there are severe limitations on who can receive multicast traffic on the Internet. Multicast should work if the sender and receivers are on the same LAN.

specifying a timeout for the receive on the UDP socket and in the `TimeLimitEchoProtocol`, using `setSoTimeout()`.

4.4.1   Keep-Alive

If no data has been exchanged for a while, each endpoint may be wondering if the other is still around. TCP provides a keep-alive mechanism where, after a certain time of inactivity, a probe message is sent to the other endpoint. If the endpoint is alive and well, it sends an acknowledgment. After a few retries without acknowledgment, the probe sender gives up and closes the socket, eliciting an exception on the next attempted I/O operation. Note that the application only sees keep-alive working if the probes *fail*.

Socket: KeepAlive

```
boolean getKeepAlive()
void setKeepAlive(boolean on)
```

   By default, keep-alive is disabled. Call the `setKeepAlive()` method with TRUE to enable keep-alive.

4.4.2   Send and Receive Buffer Size

When a `Socket` or `DatagramSocket` is created, the operating system must allocate buffers to hold incoming and outgoing data. (We talk about this in much greater detail in Section 6.1.)

Socket, DatagramSocket: Setting/Getting Send/Receive Buffer Size

```
int getReceiveBufferSize()
void setReceiveBufferSize(int size)
int getSendBufferSize()
void setSendBufferSize(int size)
```

   The getReceiveBufferSize(), setReceiveBufferSize(), getSendBufferSize(), and setSend-BufferSize() methods get and set the size (bytes) of the receive and send buffers. Note that these sizes are taken as suggestions so the actual size may not be what you specified.

   You can also specify the receive buffer size on a ServerSocket; however, this actually sets the receive buffer size for new Socket instances created by accept(). Why can you only set the receive buffer size and not the send buffer? When you accept a new Socket, it can immediately begin receiving data so you need the receive buffer size set before accept() completes the connection. On the other hand, you control when you send on a newly accepted socket, which gives you time to set the send buffer size before sending.

ServerSocket: Setting/Getting Accepted Socket Receive Buffer Size

```
int getReceiveBufferSize()
void setReceiveBufferSize(int size)
```

The getReceiveBufferSize() and setReceiveBufferSize() methods get and set the size (bytes) of the receive buffer for Socket instances created by the accept().

4.4.3 Timeout

As we've already seen, many I/O operations will block if they cannot complete immediately: reads block until at least 1 byte is available and accept blocks until a connection is initiated. Unfortunately, the blocking time is not bounded. We can specify a maximum blocking time for the various operations.

Socket, ServerSocket, DatagramSocket: Setting/Getting I/O Timeouts

```
int getSoTimeout()
void setSoTimeout(int timeout)
```

The getSoTimeout() and setSoTimeout() methods get and set the maximum time (milliseconds) to allow read/receive and accept operations to block. A timeout of 0 means the operation *never* times out. If the timeout expires, an exception is thrown.

4.4.4 Address Reuse

Under some circumstances, you may want to allow multiple sockets to bind to the same socket address. In the case of UDP multicast, you may have multiple applications on the same host participating in the same multicast group. For TCP, when a connection is closed, one (or both) endpoints must hang around for a while in "Time-Wait" state to vacuum up stray packets (see Section 6.4.2). Unfortunately, you may not be able to wait for the Time-Wait to expire. In both cases, you need the ability to bind to an address that's in use. To enable this, you must allow address reuse.

`Socket`, `ServerSocket`, `DatagramSocket`: Setting/Getting Address Reuse

```
boolean getReuseAddress()
void setReuseAddress(boolean on)
```

    The `getReuseAddress()` and `setReuseAddress()` methods get and set reuse address permissions. A value of TRUE means that address reuse is enabled.

4.4.5 Eliminating Buffering Delay

TCP attempts to help you avoid sending small packets, which waste network resources. It does this by buffering data until it has more to send. While this is good for the network, your application may not be so tolerant of this buffering delay. Fortunately, you can disable this behavior.

`Socket`: Setting/Getting TCP Buffering Delay

```
boolean getTcpNoDelay()
void setTcpNoDelay(boolean on)
```

    The `getTcpNoDelay()` and `setTcpNoDelay()` methods get and set the elimination of buffering delay. A value of TRUE means that buffering delay is disabled.

4.4.6 Urgent Data

Suppose you've sent a bunch of data to a slow receiver and suddenly you have some data that the receiver needs right now. If you send the data in the output stream, it gets queued up behind all of the regular data, and who knows when the receiver will see it? To deal with this TCP includes the concept of *urgent* data that can (theoretically) skip ahead. Such data is called out-of-band because it bypasses the normal stream.

`Socket`: Urgent Data

```
void sendUrgentData(int data)
boolean getOOBInline()
void setOOBInline(boolean on)
```

    To send urgent data, call the `sendUrgentData()` method, which sends the least significant byte of the `int` parameter. To receive this byte, the receiver must enable out-of-band data by passing TRUE to `setOOBInline()`. The byte is received in the input stream of the receiver.

Data sent before the urgent byte will precede the urgent byte in the receiver's input stream. If reception of out-of-band data is not enabled, the urgent byte is silently discarded.

Note that Java can get little use from urgent data because urgent bytes are mixed in with regular bytes *in the order of transmission*. In fact, a Java receiver cannot even tell that it's receiving urgent data.

4.4.7 Lingering after close

When you call `close()` on a socket, it immediately returns even if the socket is buffering unsent data. The problem is that your host could then fail at a later time without sending all of the data. You may optionally ask `close()` to "linger," or block, by blocking until all of the data is sent and acked or a timeout expires. See Section 6.4.2 for more details.

Socket: Linger on `close()`

```
int getSoLinger()
void setSoLinger(boolean on, int linger)
```

If you call `setSoLinger()` with on set to TRUE, then a subsequent `close()` will block until all data is acknowledged by the remote endpoint or the specified timeout (seconds) expires. If the timeout expires, the TCP connection is forceably closed. The `getSoLinger()` method returns the timeout if linger is enabled and −1 otherwise.

4.4.8 Broadcast Permission

Some operating systems require that you explicitly request permission to broadcast. You can control broadcast permissions. As you already know, `DatagramSockets` provide broadcast service.

DatagramSocket: Setting/Getting Broadcast Permissions

```
boolean getBroadcast()
void setBroadcast(boolean on)
```

The `getBroadcast()` and `setBroadcast()` methods get and set broadcast permissions. A value of TRUE means that broadcast is permitted. By default, Java permits broadcast.

4.4.9   Traffic Class

Some networks offer enhanced or "premium" services to packets classified as being eligible for the service. The *traffic class* of a packet is indicated by a value carried in the packet as it is transmitted through the network. For example, some networks might give packets in the "gold service" class higher priority, to provide reduced delay and/or reduced loss probability. Others might use the indicated traffic class to choose a route for the packet. Beware, however, that network providers charge extra for such services, so there is no guarantee these options will actually have any effect.

Socket, DatagramSocket: Setting/Getting Traffic Class

```
int getTrafficClass()
void setTrafficClass(int tc)
```

The traffic class is specified as an integer or a set of bit flags. The number and meaning of the bits depend on the version of IP you are using.

4.4.10   Performance-Based Protocol Selection

TCP may not be the only protocol available to a socket. Which protocol to use depends on what's important to your application. Java allows you to give "advice" to the implementation regarding the importance of different performance characteristics to your application. The underlying network system may use the advice to choose among different protocols that can provide equivalent stream services with different performance characteristics.

Socket, ServerSocket: Specifying Protocol Preferences

```
void setPerformancePreferences(int connectionTime, int latency, int bandwidth)
```

The performance preference for the socket is expressed by three integers representing connection time, delay, and bandwith. The specific values are not important; instead, Java compares the relative values for each criterion and returns the closest-matching, available protocol. For example, if connectionTime and latency both equal 0 and bandwidth equals 1, the protocol maximizing bandwidth will be selected. Note that this method must be called *before* the socket is connected to be effective.

4.5 Closing Connections

You've probably never given much thought to who closes a connection. In phone conversations, either side can start the process of terminating the call. It typically goes something like this:

```
"Well, I guess I'd better go."
"Ok. Bye."
"Bye."
```

Network protocols, on the other hand, are typically very specific about who "closes" first. In the echo protocol, Figure 4.1(a), the server dutifully echoes everything the client sends. When the client is finished, it calls close(). After the server has received and echoed all of the data sent before the client's call to close(), its read operation returns a −1, indicating that the client is finished. The server then calls close() on its socket. The close is a critical part of the protocol because without it the server doesn't know when the client is finished sending characters to echo. In HTTP, Figure 4.1(b), it's the server that initiates the connection close. Here, the client sends a request ("GET") to the server, and the server responds by sending a header (normally starting with "200 OK"), followed by the requested file. Since the client does not know the size of the file, the server must indicate the end-of-file by closing the socket.

Calling close() on a Socket terminates *both* directions (input and output) of data flow. (Section 6.4.2 provides a more detailed description of TCP connection termination.) Once an endpoint (client or server) closes the socket, it can no longer send *or receive* data. This means that close() can only be used to signal the other end when the caller is completely finished communicating. In the echo protocol, once the server receives the close from the client, it

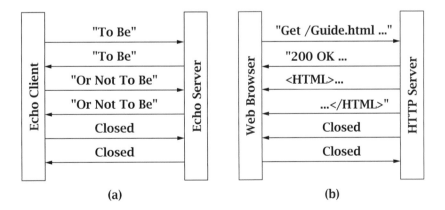

(a)   (b)

Figure 4.1: Echo (a) and HTTP (b) protocol termination.

immediately closes. In effect, the client close indicates that the communication is completed. HTTP works the same way, except that the server is the terminator.

Let's consider a different protocol. Suppose you want a compression server that takes a stream of bytes, compresses them, and sends the compressed stream back to the client. Which endpoint should close the connection? Since the stream of bytes from the client is arbitrarily long, the client needs to close the connection so that the server knows when the stream of bytes to be compressed ends. When should the client call close()? If the client calls close() on the socket immediately after it sends the last byte of data, it will not be able to receive the last bytes of compressed data. Perhaps the client could wait until it receives all of the compressed data before it closes, as the echo protocol does. Unfortunately, neither the server nor the client knows how many bytes to expect, so this will not work either. What is needed is a way to tell the other end of the connection "I am through sending," without losing the ability to receive.

Fortunately, sockets provide a way to do this. The shutdownInput() and shutdownOutput() methods of Socket allow the I/O streams to be closed independently. After shutdownInput(), the socket's input stream can no longer be used. Any undelivered data is silently discarded, and any attempt to read from the socket's input stream will return −1. After shutdownOutput() is called on a Socket, no more data may be sent on the socket's output stream. Attempts to write to the stream throw an IOException. Any data written before the call to shutdownOutput() may be read by the remote socket. After that, a read on the input stream of the remote socket will return −1. An application calling shutdownOutput can continue to read from the socket and, similarly, data can be written after calling shutdownInput.

In the compression protocol (see Figure 4.2), the client writes the bytes to be compressed, closing the output stream using shutdownOutput when finished sending, and reads the compressed byte stream from the server. The server repeatedly reads the uncompressed data and writes the compressed data until the client performs a shutdown, causing the server read to return −1, indicating an end-of-stream. The server then closes the connection and exits.

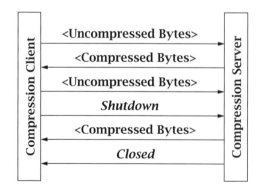

Figure 4.2: Compression protocol termination.

After the client calls shutdownOutput, it needs to read any remaining compressed bytes from the server.

Our compression client, CompressClient.java, implements the client side of the compression protocol. The uncompressed bytes are read from the file specified on the command line, and the compressed bytes are written to a new file. If the uncompressed filename is "data", the compressed filename is "data.gz". Note that this implementation works for small files, but that there is a flaw that causes deadlock for large files. (We discuss and correct this shortcoming in Section 6.2.)

CompressClient.java

```
0   import java.net.Socket;
1   import java.io.IOException;
2   import java.io.InputStream;
3   import java.io.OutputStream;
4   import java.io.FileInputStream;
5   import java.io.FileOutputStream;
6
7   /* WARNING: this code can deadlock if a large file (more than a few
8    * 10's of thousands of bytes) is sent.
9    */
10
11  public class CompressClient {
12
13    public static final int BUFSIZE = 256;  // Size of read buffer
14
15    public static void main(String[] args) throws IOException {
16
17      if (args.length != 3) { // Test for correct # of args
18        throw new IllegalArgumentException("Parameter(s): <Server> <Port> <File>");
19      }
20
21      String server = args[0];              // Server name or IP address
22      int port = Integer.parseInt(args[1]); // Server port
23      String filename = args[2];            // File to read data from
24
25      // Open input and output file (named input.gz)
26      FileInputStream fileIn = new FileInputStream(filename);
27      FileOutputStream fileOut = new FileOutputStream(filename + ".gz");
28
29      // Create socket connected to server on specified port
30      Socket sock = new Socket(server, port);
31
32      // Send uncompressed byte stream to server
```

```
33      sendBytes(sock, fileIn);
34
35      // Receive compressed byte stream from server
36      InputStream sockIn = sock.getInputStream();
37      int bytesRead;                      // Number of bytes read
38      byte[] buffer = new byte[BUFSIZE];  // Byte buffer
39      while ((bytesRead = sockIn.read(buffer)) != -1) {
40        fileOut.write(buffer, 0, bytesRead);
41        System.out.print("R");   // Reading progress indicator
42      }
43      System.out.println();      // End progress indicator line
44
45      sock.close();     // Close the socket and its streams
46      fileIn.close();   // Close file streams
47      fileOut.close();
48    }
49
50    private static void sendBytes(Socket sock, InputStream fileIn)
51        throws IOException {
52      OutputStream sockOut = sock.getOutputStream();
53      int bytesRead;                      // Number of bytes read
54      byte[] buffer = new byte[BUFSIZE];  // Byte buffer
55      while ((bytesRead = fileIn.read(buffer)) != -1) {
56        sockOut.write(buffer, 0, bytesRead);
57        System.out.print("W");   // Writing progress indicator
58      }
59      sock.shutdownOutput();     // Finished sending
60    }
61  }
```

CompressClient.java

1. **Application setup and parameter parsing:** lines 17–23

2. **Create socket and open files:** lines 25–30

3. **Invoke** sendBytes() **to transmit bytes:** line 33

4. **Receive the compressed data stream:** lines 35–42
   The while loop receives the compressed data stream and writes the bytes to the output file until an end-of-stream is signaled by a −1 from read().

5. **Close socket and file streams:** lines 45–47

6. sendBytes(): lines 50–60
   Given a socket connected to a compression server and the file input stream, read all of the uncompressed bytes from the file and write them to the socket output stream.

   ∎ **Get socket output stream:** line 52

- **Send uncompressed bytes to compression server:** lines 55–58
  The while loop reads from the input stream (in this case from a file) and repeats the bytes to the socket output stream until end-of-file, indicated by −1 from read(). Each write is indicated by a "W" printed to the console.

- **Shut down the socket output stream:** line 59
  After reading and sending all of the bytes from the input file, shut down the output stream, notifying the server that the client is finished sending. The close will cause a −1 return from read() on the server.

To implement the compression server, we simply write a protocol for our threaded server architecture. Our protocol implementation, CompressProtocol.java, implements the server-side compression protocol using the GZIP compression algorithm. The server receives the uncompressed bytes from the client and writes them to a GZIPOutputStream, which wraps the socket's output stream.

CompressProtocol.java

```
0  import java.net.Socket;
1  import java.io.IOException;
2  import java.io.InputStream;
3  import java.io.OutputStream;
4  import java.util.zip.GZIPOutputStream;
5  import java.util.logging.Logger;
6  import java.util.logging.Level;
7
8  public class CompressProtocol implements Runnable {
9
10   public static final int BUFSIZE = 1024;   // Size of receive buffer
11   private Socket clntSock;
12   private Logger logger;
13
14   public CompressProtocol(Socket clntSock, Logger logger) {
15     this.clntSock = clntSock;
16     this.logger = logger;
17   }
18
19   public static void handleCompressClient(Socket clntSock, Logger logger) {
20     try {
21       // Get the input and output streams from socket
22       InputStream in = clntSock.getInputStream();
23       GZIPOutputStream out = new GZIPOutputStream(clntSock.getOutputStream());
24
25       byte[] buffer = new byte[BUFSIZE];   // Allocate read/write buffer
26       int bytesRead;                       // Number of bytes read
```

```
27        // Receive until client closes connection, indicated by -1 return
28        while ((bytesRead = in.read(buffer)) != -1)
29          out.write(buffer, 0, bytesRead);
30        out.finish();       // Flush bytes from GZIPOutputStream
31
32        logger.info("Client " + clntSock.getRemoteSocketAddress() + " finished");
33      } catch (IOException ex) {
34        logger.log(Level.WARNING, "Exception in echo protocol", ex);
35      }
36
37      try {  // Close socket
38        clntSock.close();
39      } catch (IOException e) {
40        logger.info("Exception = " + e.getMessage());
41      }
42    }
43
44    public void run() {
45      handleCompressClient(this.clntSock, this.logger);
46    }
47  }
```

CompressProtocol.java

1. **Variables and constructors:** lines 10–17
2. handleCompressClient(): lines 19–42
   Given a socket connected to the compression client, read the uncompressed bytes from the client and write the compressed bytes back.
   - **Get socket I/O streams:** lines 22–23
     The socket's output stream is wrapped in a GZIPOutputStream. The sequence of bytes written to this stream is compressed, using the GZIP algorithm, before being written to the underlying output stream.
   - **Read uncompressed and write compressed bytes:** lines 28–29
     The while loop reads from the socket input stream and writes to the GZIPOutputStream, which in turn writes to the socket output stream, until the end-of-stream indication is received.
   - **Flush and close:** lines 30–42
     Calling finish on the GZIPOutputStream is necessary to flush any bytes that may be buffered by the compression algorithm.
   - run() **method:** lines 44–46
     The run() method simply calls the handleCompressClient() method.

To use this protocol we simply modify TCPEchoServerExecutor.java to create an instance of CompressProtocol instead of EchoProtocol:

```
service.execute(new CompressProtocol(clntSock, logger));
```

4.6 Applets

Applets can perform network communication using TCP/IP sockets, but there are severe restrictions on how and with whom they can converse. Without such restrictions, unsuspecting Web browsers might execute malicious applets that could, for example, send fake email, attempt to hack other systems while the browser user gets the blame, and so on. These security restrictions are enforced by the Java security manager, and violations by the applet result in a SecurityException. Typically, browsers only allow applets to communicate with the host that served the applet. This means that applets are usually restricted to communicating with applications executing on that host, usually a Web server originating the applet. The list of security restrictions and general applet programming is beyond the scope of this book. It is worth noting, however, that the default security restrictions can be altered, if allowed by the browser user.

Suppose that you wanted to implement an applet that allowed users to type and save notes to themselves on their browser. Browser security restrictions prevent applets from saving data directly on the local file system, so you would need some other means besides local disk I/O to save the notes. FileClientApplet.java (available from the book's Web site) is an applet that allows the user to type text into an editor window and, by clicking the "Save" button, copy the text over the network to a server (running on port 5000). The server, TCPFileServer.java (also on the book's Web site), saves the data to a file. It takes a port (use 5000 to work with the applet) and the name of the file. The server must execute on the Web server that serves the applet to the browser. Note that there is nothing applet-specific about the server. FileClientApplet.html on the Web site demonstrates how to integrate the applet into a Web page.

4.7 Wrapping Up

We have discussed some of the ways Java provides access to advanced features of the sockets API, and how built-in features such as threads and executors can be used with socket programs. In addition to these facilities, Java provides several mechanisms (not discussed here) that operate on top of TCP or UDP and attempt to hide the complexity of protocol development. For example, Java Remote Method Invocation (RMI) allows Java objects on different hosts to invoke one another's methods as if the objects all reside locally. The URL class and associated classes provide a framework for developing Web-related programs. Many other standard Java library mechanisms exist, providing an amazing range of services. These mechanisms are beyond the scope of this book; however, we encourage you to look at the book's Web site for descriptions and code examples for some of these libraries.

4.8 Exercises

1. State precisely the conditions under which an iterative server is preferable to a multiprocessing server.

2. Would you ever need to implement a timeout in a client or server that uses TCP?

3. How can you determine the minimum and maximum allowable sizes for a socket's send and receive buffers? Determine the minimums for your system.

4. Modify TCPEchoClient.java so that it closes its output side of the connection before attempting to receive any echoed data.

chapter **5**

NIO

This chapter introduces the main facilities of the "New I/O" packages. There are two important parts: the **java.nio.channels** package, which introduces the Selector and Channel abstractions, and the **java.nio** package, which introduces the Buffer abstraction. These are fairly advanced features, with a number of subtle details related to their usage. Therefore this chapter is organized a little differently than the earlier ones. In the first subsection we'll motivate the NIO features by describing some problems that they are intended to solve— specifically, challenges that arise in building high-performance servers without them. (If you don't care about the "why?" question, feel free to skip this section.) In Section 5.2, we present (as usual) a client for the (TCP) "echo" protocol that shows the use of SocketChannel and Buffer classes, as well as the nonblocking features of Channel, which differ from those we saw in Section 4.2. In Section 5.3, we show a server that uses the Selector, Channel, and Buffer abstractions. Then we go back and cover the details of usage of the main abstractions, each in its own section. Finally, Section 5.7 introduces the DatagramChannel class (the channelized version of DatagramSocket).

5.1 Why Do We Need This?

Basic Java Sockets work well for small-scale systems. But when it comes to servers that have to deal with many thousands of clients simultaneously, certain issues arise. We saw signs of this in Chapter 4: the thread-per-client approach is limited in terms of scalability because of the overhead associated with creating, maintaining, and swapping between threads. Using a thread *pool* saves on that kind of overhead while still allowing an implementor to take advantage of parallel hardware, but for protocols with long-lived connections, the size of the thread pool still limits the number of clients that can be handled simultaneously. Consider an instant messaging server that relays messages between clients. Clients must be continuously connected to receive messages, so the thread pool size limits the total number of clients that can be served. Increasing the thread pool size increases the thread-handling overhead without improving performance, because most of the time clients are idle.

If this were all there is to it, NIO might not be needed. Unfortunately, there are other, more subtle challenges involved with using threads for scalability. One is that the programmer has very little control over *which* threads receive service *when*. You can set a Thread instance's *priority* (higher-priority threads get preference over lower-priority ones), but ultimately the priority is just "advice"—which thread is chosen to run next is entirely up to the implementation.[1] Thus, if a programmer wants to ensure that certain connections get served before others, or impose a specific order of service, threads may make it harder to do that.

But the most important issue with threads is probably one we haven't encountered yet. That's because in our "echo service" examples, each client served is completely independent of all others; clients do not interact with each other or affect the state of the server. However, some (most) servers have some information—what we call "state"—that needs to be accessed or modified by different clients at the same time. Think of a service that allows citizens to reserve parking spaces for one-hour blocks in a big city, for example. The schedule of who gets which space for which time blocks must be kept consistent; the server may also need to ensure that the same user does not reserve more than one space at a time. These constraints require that some state information (i.e., the schedule) be shared across all clients. This in turn requires that access to that state be carefully *synchronized* through the use of *locks* or other mutual exclusion mechanisms. Otherwise, since the scheduler can interleave program steps from different threads more or less arbitrarily, different threads that are trying to update the schedule concurrently might overwrite each other's changes.

The need to synchronize access to shared state makes it significantly harder to think about both correctness and performance of a threaded server. The reasons for this added complexity are beyond the scope of this book, but suffice it to say that the use of the required synchronization mechanisms adds still more scheduling and context-switching overhead, over which the programmer has essentially no control.

Because of these complications, some programmers prefer to stick with a *single-threaded* approach, in which the server has only one thread, which deals with all clients—not sequentially, but all at once. Such a server cannot afford to block on an I/O operation with any one client, and must use *nonblocking I/O* exclusively. Recall that with nonblocking I/O, we

---

[1]One of the "official" reference books on Java says it this way: "There are no guarantees, only a general expectation that preference is typically given to running higher-priority threads.... Do not rely on thread priority for algorithm correctness" [1], pages 358–359.

specify the maximum amount of time that a call to an I/O method may block (including zero). We saw an example of this in Chapter 4, where we set a timeout on the accept operation (via the setSoTimeout() method of ServerSocket). When we call accept() on that ServerSocket instance, if a new connection is pending, accept() returns immediately; otherwise it blocks until either a connection comes in or the timer expires, whichever comes first. This allows a single thread to handle multiple connections. Unfortunately, the approach requires that we constantly *poll* all sources of I/O, and that kind of "busy waiting" approach again introduces a lot of overhead from cycling through connections just to find out that they have nothing to do.

What we need is a way to poll a *set of clients all at once*, to find out which ones need service. That is exactly the point of the Selector and Channel abstractions introduced in NIO. A Channel instance represents a "pollable" I/O target such as a socket (or a file, or a device). Channels can *register* an instance of class Selector. The select() method of Selector allows you to ask "Among the set of channels, which ones are currently ready to be serviced (i.e., accepted, read, or written)?" There are numerous details to be covered later, but that's the basic motivation for Selector and Channel, both of which are part of the java.nio.channels package.

The other major feature introduced in NIO is the Buffer class. Just as selectors and channels give greater control and predictability of the overhead involved with handling many clients at once, Buffer enables more efficient, predictable I/O than is possible with the Stream abstraction. The nice thing about the stream abstraction is that it hides the finiteness of the underlying buffering, providing the illusion of an arbitrary-length container. The bad thing is that implementing that illusion may require either lots of memory allocation or lots of context-switching, or both. As with threads, this overhead is buried in the implementation, and is therefore not controllable or predictable. That approach makes it easy to write programs, but harder to tune their performance. Unfortunately, if you use the Java Socket abstraction, streams are all you've got.

That's why channels are designed around the use of Buffer instances to pass data around. The Buffer abstraction represents a *finite-capacity* container for data—essentially, an array with associated pointers indicating where to put data in, and where to read data out. There are two main advantages to using Buffer. First, the overhead associated with reading from and writing to the buffer is exposed to the programmer. For example, if you want to put data into a buffer but there's not enough room, you have to do something to make more room (i.e., get some data out, or move data that's already there to make more room, or create a new instance). This represents extra work, but you (the programmer) control how, whether, and when it happens. A smart programmer, who knows the application requirements well, can often reduce overhead by tweaking these choices. Second, some specialized flavors of Buffer map operations on the Java object directly to operations on resources of the underlying platform (for example, to buffers in the operating system). This saves some copying of data between different address spaces—an expensive operation on modern architectures.

5.2 Using Channels with Buffers

As we said above, a Channel instance represents a connection to a device through which we can perform I/O. In fact the basic ideas are very similar to what we've already seen with plain sockets. For TCP, use the ServerSocketChannel and SocketChannel. There are other types of channels for other devices (e.g., FileChannel), and most of what we say here applies to them as well, although we do not mention them further. One difference between channels and sockets is that typically one obtains a channel instance by calling a static factory method:

```
SocketChannel clntChan = SocketChannel.open();
ServerSocketChannel servChan = ServerSocketChannel.open();
```

Channels do not use streams; instead, they send/receive data from/to buffers. An instance of Buffer or any of its subclasses can be viewed as a fixed-length sequence of elements of a single primitive Java type. Unlike streams, buffers have fixed, finite capacity, and internal (but accessible) state that keeps track of how much data has been put in or taken out; they behave something like queues with finite capacity. The Buffer class is abstract; you get a buffer by creating an instance of one of its subtypes, each of which is designed to hold one of the primitive Java types (with the exception of boolean). Thus each instance is a FloatBuffer, or an IntBuffer, or a ByteBuffer, etc. (The ByteBuffer is the most flexible of these and will be used in most of our examples.) As with channels, constructors are not typically used to create buffer instances; instead they are created either by calling allocate(), specifying a capacity:

```
ByteBuffer buffer = ByteBuffer.allocate(CAPACITY);
```

or by wrapping an existing array:

```
ByteBuffer buffer = ByteBuffer.wrap(byteArray);
```

Part of the power of NIO comes from the fact that channels can be made nonblocking. Recall that some socket operations can block indefinitely. For example, a call to accept() can block waiting for a client to connect; a call to read() can block until data arrives from the other end of a connection. In general, I/O calls that make/accept a connection or read/write data can block indefinitely until something happens in the underlying network implementations. A slow, lossy, or just plain broken network can cause an arbitrary delay. Unfortunately, in general we don't know if a method call will block before we make it. An important feature of the NIO channel abstraction is that we can make a channel nonblocking by configuring its blocking behavior:

```
clntChan.configureBlocking(false);
```

Calls to methods on a nonblocking channel always return immediately. The return value of such a call indicates the extent to which the requested operation was achieved.

For example, a call to accept() on a nonblocking ServerSocketChannel returns the client SocketChannel if a connection is pending and null otherwise.

Let's construct a nonblocking TCP echo client. The I/O operations that may block include connecting, reading, and writing. With a nonblocking channel, these operations return immediately. We must repeatedly call these operations until we have successfully completed all I/O.

TCPEchoClientNonblocking.java

```
0   import java.net.InetSocketAddress;
1   import java.net.SocketException;
2   import java.nio.ByteBuffer;
3   import java.nio.channels.SocketChannel;
4
5   public class TCPEchoClientNonblocking {
6
7     public static void main(String args[]) throws Exception {
8
9       if ((args.length < 2) || (args.length > 3)) // Test for correct # of args
10        throw new IllegalArgumentException("Parameter(s): <Server> <Word> [<Port>]");
11
12      String server = args[0]; // Server name or IP address
13      // Convert input String to bytes using the default charset
14      byte[] argument = args[1].getBytes();
15
16      int servPort = (args.length == 3) ? Integer.parseInt(args[2]) : 7;
17
18      // Create channel and set to nonblocking
19      SocketChannel clntChan = SocketChannel.open();
20      clntChan.configureBlocking(false);
21
22      // Initiate connection to server and repeatedly poll until complete
23      if (!clntChan.connect(new InetSocketAddress(server, servPort))) {
24        while (!clntChan.finishConnect()) {
25          System.out.print(".");  // Do something else
26        }
27      }
28      ByteBuffer writeBuf = ByteBuffer.wrap(argument);
29      ByteBuffer readBuf = ByteBuffer.allocate(argument.length);
30      int totalBytesRcvd = 0; // Total bytes received so far
31      int bytesRcvd; // Bytes received in last read
32      while (totalBytesRcvd < argument.length) {
33        if (writeBuf.hasRemaining()) {
```

```
34          clntChan.write(writeBuf);
35        }
36        if ((bytesRcvd = clntChan.read(readBuf)) == -1) {
37          throw new SocketException("Connection closed prematurely");
38        }
39        totalBytesRcvd += bytesRcvd;
40        System.out.print(".");   // Do something else
41      }
42
43      System.out.println("Received: " +  // convert to String per default charset
44          new String(readBuf.array(), 0, totalBytesRcvd));
45      clntChan.close();
46    }
47  }
```

TCPEchoClientNonblocking.java

1. **Get and convert arguments:** lines 9–16

2. **Create nonblocking** SocketChannel: lines 19–20

3. **Connect to server:** lines 23–27
   Because the socket is nonblocking, the call to connect() may return before the connection is established; the method returns TRUE if the connection completes before it returns, FALSE otherwise. In the latter case, any attempt to send/receive will throw a NotYetConnect-edException, so we "poll" the status continually by calling finishConnect(), which returns FALSE until the connection completes. The print operation demonstrates that we can perform other tasks while waiting for the connection to complete. Such a busy wait is generally wasteful; we do it here to illustrate the use of the methods.

4. **Create read/write buffers:** lines 28–29
   We create the ByteBuffer instances we'll use for writing and reading by wrapping the byte[] containing the string we want to send, and allocating a new instance the same size as that array, respectively.

5. **Loop until we have sent and received all the bytes:** lines 32–41
   Call write() as long as the output buffer has anything left in it. The call to read() does not block but rather returns 0 when no data is available to return. Again, the print operation demonstrates that we can perform other tasks while waiting for the communication to complete.

6. **Print the received data:** lines 43–44

7. **Close the channel:** line 45
   Like sockets, channels should be closed when they are no longer needed.

5.3 Selectors

As noted in the first section of this chapter, the Selector class allows us to avoid the wasteful "busy waiting" approach we saw in the nonblocking client. Consider an Instant Messaging server, for example. Thousands of clients may be connected, but only a few (possibly none) have messages waiting to be read and relayed at any time. We need a way to block just until at least one channel is ready for I/O, and to tell which channels are ready. NIO selectors do all of this. An instance of Selector can simultaneously check (and wait, if desired) for I/O opportunities on a set of channels. In technical terms, a selector is a multiplexor because a single selector can manage I/O on multiple channels.

To use a selector, create it (using the static factory method open()) and *register* it with the channels that you wish to monitor (note that this is done via a method of the *channel*, not the selector). Finally, call the selector's select() method, which blocks until one or more channels are ready for I/O or a timeout expires. When select() returns, it tells you the number of channels ready for I/O. Now, in a single thread, we can check for ready I/O on several channels by calling select(). If no I/O becomes ready after a certain amount of time, select() returns 0 and allows us to continue on with other tasks.

Let's look at an example. Suppose we want to implement an echo server using channels and a selector without using multiple threads or busy waiting. To make it easier to use this basic server pattern with different protocols, we have factored out the protocol-specific details of how each type of I/O (accepting, reading, and writing) is handled through the channel. TCPProtocol defines the interface between the generic TCPSelectorServer.java and the specific protocol. It includes three methods, one for each form of I/O; the server simply invokes the appropriate method once a channel becomes ready.

TCPProtocol.java

```
0   import java.nio.channels.SelectionKey;
1   import java.io.IOException;
2
3   public interface TCPProtocol {
4     void handleAccept(SelectionKey key) throws IOException;
5     void handleRead(SelectionKey key) throws IOException;
6     void handleWrite(SelectionKey key) throws IOException;
7   }
```

TCPProtocol.java

Now for the server. We create a selector and register it with a ServerSocketChannel for each socket on which the server listens for incoming client connections. Then we loop forever, invoking select(), and calling the appropriate handler routine for whatever type of I/O is appropriate.

TCPServerSelector.java

```
0   import java.io.IOException;
1   import java.net.InetSocketAddress;
2   import java.nio.channels.SelectionKey;
3   import java.nio.channels.Selector;
4   import java.nio.channels.ServerSocketChannel;
5   import java.util.Iterator;
6
7   public class TCPServerSelector {
8
9     private static final int BUFSIZE = 256;  // Buffer size (bytes)
10    private static final int TIMEOUT = 3000; // Wait timeout (milliseconds)
11
12    public static void main(String[] args) throws IOException {
13
14      if (args.length < 1) { // Test for correct # of args
15        throw new IllegalArgumentException("Parameter(s): <Port> ...");
16      }
17
18      // Create a selector to multiplex listening sockets and connections
19      Selector selector = Selector.open();
20
21      // Create listening socket channel for each port and register selector
22      for (String arg : args) {
23        ServerSocketChannel listnChannel = ServerSocketChannel.open();
24        listnChannel.socket().bind(new InetSocketAddress(Integer.parseInt(arg)));
25        listnChannel.configureBlocking(false); // must be nonblocking to register
26        // Register selector with channel. The returned key is ignored
27        listnChannel.register(selector, SelectionKey.OP_ACCEPT);
28      }
29
30      // Create a handler that will implement the protocol
31      TCPProtocol protocol = new EchoSelectorProtocol(BUFSIZE);
32
33      while (true) { // Run forever, processing available I/O operations
34        // Wait for some channel to be ready (or timeout)
35        if (selector.select(TIMEOUT) == 0) { // returns # of ready chans
36          System.out.print(".");
37          continue;
38        }
39
```

```
40      // Get iterator on set of keys with I/O to process
41      Iterator<SelectionKey> keyIter = selector.selectedKeys().iterator();
42      while (keyIter.hasNext()) {
43        SelectionKey key = keyIter.next(); // Key is bit mask
44        // Server socket channel has pending connection requests?
45        if (key.isAcceptable()) {
46          protocol.handleAccept(key);
47        }
48        // Client socket channel has pending data?
49        if (key.isReadable()) {
50          protocol.handleRead(key);
51        }
52        // Client socket channel is available for writing and
53        // key is valid (i.e., channel not closed)?
54        if (key.isValid() && key.isWritable()) {
55          protocol.handleWrite(key);
56        }
57        keyIter.remove(); // remove from set of selected keys
58      }
59    }
60   }
61 }
```

TCPServerSelector.java

1. **Setup:** lines 14–19
   Verify at least one argument, create a Selector instance.

2. **Create a ServerSocketChannel for each port:** lines 22–28
   - **Create a ServerSocketChannel:** line 23
   - **Make it listen on the given port:** line 24
     We have to fetch the underlying ServerSocket and invoke its bind() method on the port given as argument. Any argument other than a number in the appropriate range will result in an IOException.
   - **Make it nonblocking:** line 25
     Only nonblocking channels can register selectors, so we configure the blocking state appropriately.
   - **Register selector with channel:** line 27
     We indicate our interest in the "accept" operation during registration.

3. **Create protocol handler:** line 31
   To get access to the handler methods for the Echo protocol, we create an instance of the EchoSelectorProtocol, which exports the required methods.

4. **Loop forever, waiting for I/O, invoking handler:** lines 33–59

■ **Select:** line 35
This version of the select() method blocks until some channel becomes ready or until the timeout expires. It returns the number of ready channels; zero indicates that the timeout expired, in which case we print a dot to mark the passage of time and iterate.

■ **Get selected key set:** line 41
The selectedKeys() method returns a Set, for which we get an Iterator. The set contains the SelectionKey (created at registration time) of each channel that is ready for one of the I/O operations of interest (specified at registration time).

■ **Iterate over keys, checking ready operations:** lines 42–58
For each key, we check whether it is ready for accept(), readable, and/or writable, invoking the appropriate handler method to perform the indicated operation in each case.

■ **Remove the key from the set:** line 57
The select() operation only *adds* to the set of selected keys associated with a Selector. Therefore if we do not remove each key as we process it, it will *remain* in the set across the next call to select(), and a useless operation may be invoked on it.

TCPServerSelector is protocol agnostic for the most part; only the single line of code assigning the value of protocol is protocol-specific. All protocol details are contained in the implementation of the TCPProtocol interface. EchoSelectorProtocol provides an implementation of the handlers for the Echo protocol. You could easily write your own protocol handlers for other protocols or performance improvements on our Echo protocol handler implementation.

EchoSelectorProtocol.java

```
0   import java.nio.channels.SelectionKey;
1   import java.nio.channels.SocketChannel;
2   import java.nio.channels.ServerSocketChannel;
3   import java.nio.ByteBuffer;
4   import java.io.IOException;
5
6   public class EchoSelectorProtocol implements TCPProtocol {
7
8     private int bufSize; // Size of I/O buffer
9
10    public EchoSelectorProtocol(int bufSize) {
11      this.bufSize = bufSize;
12    }
13
14    public void handleAccept(SelectionKey key) throws IOException {
15      SocketChannel clntChan = ((ServerSocketChannel) key.channel()).accept();
16      clntChan.configureBlocking(false); // Must be nonblocking to register
17      // Register the selector with new channel for read and attach byte buffer
```

```
18        clntChan.register(key.selector(), SelectionKey.OP_READ, ByteBuffer.allocate(bufSize));
19
20    }
21
22    public void handleRead(SelectionKey key) throws IOException {
23      // Client socket channel has pending data
24      SocketChannel clntChan = (SocketChannel) key.channel();
25      ByteBuffer buf = (ByteBuffer) key.attachment();
26      long bytesRead = clntChan.read(buf);
27      if (bytesRead == -1) { // Did the other end close?
28        clntChan.close();
29      } else if (bytesRead > 0) {
30        // Indicate via key that reading/writing are both of interest now.
31        key.interestOps(SelectionKey.OP_READ | SelectionKey.OP_WRITE);
32      }
33    }
34
35    public void handleWrite(SelectionKey key) throws IOException {
36      /*
37       * Channel is available for writing, and key is valid (i.e., client channel
38       * not closed).
39       */
40      // Retrieve data read earlier
41      ByteBuffer buf = (ByteBuffer) key.attachment();
42      buf.flip(); // Prepare buffer for writing
43      SocketChannel clntChan = (SocketChannel) key.channel();
44      clntChan.write(buf);
45      if (!buf.hasRemaining()) { // Buffer completely written?
46        // Nothing left, so no longer interested in writes
47        key.interestOps(SelectionKey.OP_READ);
48      }
49      buf.compact(); // Make room for more data to be read in
50    }
51
52  }
```

EchoSelectorProtocol.java

1. **Declaration of implementation of the** TCPProtocol **interface:** line 6

2. **Member variables and constructor:** lines 8-12
   Each instance contains the size of buffer to be created for each client channel.

3. handleAccept(): lines 14-20

   ■ **Get channel from key and accept connection:** line 15
     The channel() method returns the Channel that created the key at registration time. (We
     know it's a ServerSocketChannel because that's the only kind we registered with that

supports the "accept" operation.) The accept() method returns a SocketChannel for the incoming connection.

- ■ **Make nonblocking:** line 16
  Again, we cannot register with a blocking channel.

- ■ **Register selector with channel:** lines 18-19
  As with the channel, we can retrieve the Selector associated with the SelectionKey via its selector() method. We create a new ByteBuffer of the required size, and pass it as argument to register(). It will be associated as an attachment to the SelectionKey instance returned by the register() method. (We ignore the returned key now, but will access it through the selected keys set if the channel becomes ready for I/O.)

4. handleRead(): lines 22-33

- ■ **Get channel associated with key:** line 24
  We know this is a SocketChannel because it supports reading.

- ■ **Get buffer associated with key:** line 25
  When the connection was associated, a ByteBuffer was attached to this SelectionKey instance.

- ■ **Read from the channel:** line 27

- ■ **Check for end of stream and close channel:** lines 27-28
  If the read() returns −1, we know the underlying connection closed, and close the channel in that case. Closing the channel removes its associated key from the selector's various sets.

- ■ **If data received, indicate interest in writing:** lines 29-31
  Note that we are still interested in reading, although there may not be any room left in the buffer.

5. handleWrite(): lines 35-50

- ■ **Retrieve buffer containing received data:** line 41
  The ByteBuffer attached to the given SelectionKey contains data read earlier from the channel.

- ■ **Prepare buffer for writing:** line 42
  The Buffer's internal state indicates where to *put data next*, and how much *space* is left. The flip() operation modifies the state so it indicates from where to *get* data for the write() operation, and how much *data* is left. (This is explained in detail in the next section.) The effect is that the write operation will start consuming the data produced by the earlier read.

- ■ **Get channel:** line 43

- ■ **Write to channel:** line 44

- ■ **If buffer empty, lose interest in writing:** lines 45-48
  If there is no received data left in the buffer, we modify the interest set associated with the key so that it indicates only read is of interest.

■ **Compact the buffer:** line 49

If there is data remaining in the buffer, this operation moves it to the front of the buffer so more data can be read on the next iteration (semantics of this operation are covered in more detail in Section 5.4.5). In any case, the operation resets the state so the buffer is again ready for reading. Note that the buffer associated with a channel is always set up for reading except when control is inside the `handleWrite()` method.

We are now ready to delve into the details of the three main NIO abstractions.

5.4 Buffers in Detail

As you've already seen, in NIO data is read into and written from buffers. Channels read data into buffers. We then access the data through the buffer. To write data, we first fill the buffer with data in the order we wish to send it. Basically, a buffer is just a list where all of the elements are a single primitive type (typically bytes). A buffer is fixed-length; it cannot expand like some other classes (e.g., `List`, `StringBuffer`, etc). Note that `ByteBuffer` is commonly used because 1) it provides methods for reading and writing other types, and 2) the channel read/write methods accept only `ByteBuffers`. So what good are `IntBuffer`, `DoubleBuffer`, and the others? Stay tuned! The answer will be revealed in Section 5.4.6.

5.4.1 Buffer Indices

A buffer goes beyond just storing a list of elements. It has internal state that keeps track of the current position when reading data from or writing data to the buffer, as well as the end of valid data for reading, etc. To do this, each buffer maintains four indices into its list of elements; they are shown in Table 5.1. (We'll see shortly how the indices are modified by the various buffer methods.)

Index	Description	Accessor/Mutator/Usage
capacity	Number of elements in buffer (Immutable)	`int capacity()`
position	Next element to read/write (numbered from 0)	`int position()` `Buffer position(int newPosition)`
limit	First unreadable/unwritable element	`int limit()` `Buffer limit(int newLimit)`
mark	User-chosen prev. value of *position*, or 0	`Buffer mark()` `Buffer reset()`

Table 5.1: Buffer Internal State

The distance between the *position* and *limit* tells us the number of bytes available for getting/putting. Java provides two convenience methods for evaluating this distance.

ByteBuffer: Remaining Bytes

```
boolean hasRemaining()
int remaining()
```

hasRemaining() returns TRUE if at least one element is available, and remaining() returns the number of elements available.

The following relationships among these variables are maintained as an invariant:

$$0 \le mark \le position \le limit \le capacity$$

The *mark* value "remembers" a position so you can come back to it later; the reset() method returns the *position* to the value it had when mark() was last called (unless doing so would violate the above invariant).

5.4.2 Buffer Creation

Typically, we create buffers either by allocation or by wrapping an array of primitives. The static factory methods for creating a ByteBuffer are shown in Table 5.2, along with the initial values of *capacity*, *position*, and *limit* for the returned instance. The initial value of *mark* is undefined for all newly created Buffer instances; attempts to reset() the *position* before calling mark() result in an InvalidMarkException.

To allocate a fresh instance, we simply call the static allocate() method for the type of buffer we want, specifying the number of elements:

```
ByteBuffer byteBuf = ByteBuffer.allocate(20);
DoubleBuffer dblBuf = DoubleBuffer.allocate(5);
```

Method	Capacity	Position	Limit
ByteBuffer allocate(int capacity)	*capacity*	0	*capacity*
ByteBuffer allocateDirect(int capacity)	*capacity*	0	*capacity*
ByteBuffer wrap(byte[] array)	array.length	0	array.length
ByteBuffer wrap(byte[] array, int offset, int length)	array.length	offset	offset + length

Table 5.2: ByteBuffer Creation Methods

Here byteBuf holds 20 bytes, and dblBuf holds 5 Java doubles. These buffers are fixed-size so they can never be expanded or contracted. If you find that the buffer you just allocated is too short, your only option is to allocate a new, correctly sized buffer.

We can also create a buffer from an existing array by calling the static wrap() method and passing the array to be wrapped

```
byteArray[] = new byte[BUFFERSIZE];
// ...Fill array...
ByteBuffer byteWrap = ByteBuffer.wrap(byteArray);
ByteBuffer subByteWrap = ByteBuffer.wrap(byteArray, 3, 3);
```

A buffer created by wrapping contains the data from the wrapped array. In fact, wrap() simply creates a buffer with a reference to the wrapped array, called the backing array. Any change to the data in the backing array changes the data in the buffer and vice versa. If we specify an offset and length to wrap(), the buffer is backed by the entire array with position and limit initially set to offset and offset + length. The elements preceding the offset and following the length are still accessible via the buffer.

Creation of a buffer by allocation isn't really so different from wrapping. The only real difference is that allocate() creates its own backing array. You can get a reference to this backing array by calling array() on the buffer. You can even get the offset into the backing array of the first element used by the buffer by calling arrayOffset(). A buffer created with wrap() with a nonzero offset still has an array offset of 0.

So far, all of our buffers store data in Java-allocated backing arrays. Typically, the underlying platform (operating system) cannot use these buffers to perform I/O. Instead the OS must use its own buffers for I/O and copy the results to/from the buffer's backing array. Such copying can get expensive, especially if there are many reads and writes requiring copying. Java NIO provides *direct buffers* as a way around this problem. With a direct buffer, Java allocates the backing store of the buffer from storage that the platform can use for I/O directly, so copying is unnecessary. Such low-level, native I/O generally operates at the byte level, so only ByteBuffers can be directly allocated.

```
ByteBuffer byteBufDirect = ByteBuffer.allocateDirect(BUFFERSIZE);
```

You can test whether a buffer is direct by calling isDirect(). Since a direct buffer does not have a backing array, calling array() or arrayOffset() on a direct buffer will throw an UnsupportedOperationException. There are a few caveats to remember when considering whether to use direct buffers. Calling allocateDirect() doesn't guarantee you are allocated a direct buffer—your platform or JVM may not support this operation, so you have to call isDirect() after attempting to allocate. Also, allocation and deallocation of a direct buffer is typically more expensive than for nondirect buffers, because the backing store of a direct buffer typically lives outside the JVM, requiring interaction with the operating system for management. Consequently, you should only allocate direct buffers when they will be used for a long time, over many I/O operations. In fact, it is a good idea to use direct buffers only if they provide a measurable increase in performance over nondirect buffers.

5.4.3 Storing and Retrieving Data

Once you have a buffer, it's time to use it to hold data. As "containers" for data, buffers are used for both input and output; this is different from streams, which transfer data in only one direction. We place data into a buffer using put(), and retrieve data from a buffer using get(). A channel read() implicitly calls put(), and a channel write() implicitly calls get() on the given buffer. Below we present the get() and put() methods for ByteBuffer; however, the other buffer types have similar methods.

┌── **ByteBuffer**: **Getting and putting bytes** ──────────────────────────────────┐

Relative:
byte get()
ByteBuffer get(byte[] dst)
ByteBuffer get(byte[] dst, int offset, int length)
ByteBuffer put(byte b)
ByteBuffer put(byte[] src)
ByteBuffer put(byte[] src, int offset, int length)
ByteBuffer put(ByteBuffer src)
Absolute:
byte get(int index)
ByteBuffer put(int index, byte b)

There are two types of get() and put(): relative and absolute. The relative variants get/put data from/to the "next" location in the buffer according to the value of *position*, and then increment *position* by an appropriate amount (that is, by one for the single-byte form, by array.length for the array form, and by length for the array/offset/length form). Thus, each call to put() appends after elements already contained in the buffer, and each call to get() retrieves the next element from the buffer. However, if doing so would cause *position* to go past *limit*, a get() throws a BufferUnderflowException, while a put() throws a BufferOverflowException. For example, if the destination array passed to get() is longer than the available remaining elements in the buffer, get() throws BufferUnderflowException; partial gets/puts are not allowed. The absolute variants of get() and put() take a specific index for getting and putting data; *the absolute forms do not modify position*. They do, however, throw IndexOutOfBoundsException if the given index exceeds *limit*.

└──┘

The class ByteBuffer provides additional methods for relative and absolute get/put of other types besides bytes; in this way, it's like a DataOutputStream.

┌── **ByteBuffer**: **Getting and putting Java multibyte primitives** ──────────────┐

⟨*type*⟩ get⟨*Type*⟩()
⟨*type*⟩ get⟨*Type*⟩(int index)

```
ByteBuffer put⟨Type⟩(⟨type⟩ value)
ByteBuffer put⟨Type⟩(int index, ⟨type⟩ value)
```
where "⟨Type⟩" stands for one of Char, Double, Int, Long, Short
and "⟨type⟩" stands for one of char, double, int, long, short

Each call to a relative put() or get() advances the value of *position* by the length of the particular parameter type: 2 for short, 4 for int, etc. However, if doing so would cause *position* to exceed *limit*, a BufferUnderflowException (get) or BufferOverflowException (put) is thrown: partial gets and puts are not allowed. In the case of under/overflow, position does not change.

You may have noticed that many get/put methods return a ByteBuffer. In fact, they return the same instance of ByteBuffer that was passed as an argument. This allows *call chaining*, where the result of the first call is used to make a subsequent call. For example, we can put the integers 1 and 2 in the ByteBuffer instance *myBuffer* as follows:

```
myBuffer.putInt(1).putInt(2);
```

Recall from Chapter 3 that multibyte values have a byte order, namely big- or little-endian. By default Java uses big-endian. You can get and set the order in which multibyte values are written to a byte buffer, using the built-in instances ByteOrder.BIG_ENDIAN and ByteOrder.LITTLE_ENDIAN.

`ByteBuffer`: Byte ordering in buffer

```
ByteOrder order()
ByteBuffer order(ByteOrder order)
```

The first method returns the buffer's current byte order, as one of the constants of the ByteOrder class. The second allows you to set the byte order used to write multibyte quantities.

Let's look at an example using byte order:

```
ByteBuffer buffer = ByteBuffer.allocate(4);
buffer.putShort((short) 1);
buffer.order(ByteOrder.LITTLE_ENDIAN);
buffer.putShort((short) 1);
// Predict the byte values for buffer and test your prediction
```

With all of this talk about byte ordering, you may be wondering about the byte order of your processor. ByteOrder defines a method to answer your question:

┌─ **ByteOrder:** Finding byte order ─────────────────────────────┐

```
static final ByteOrder BIG_ENDIAN
static final ByteOrder LITTLE_ENDIAN
static ByteOrder nativeOrder()
```

The method nativeOrder() returns one of the two constants BIG_ENDIAN or LITTLE_ENDIAN.

└──┘

5.4.4   Preparing Buffers: clear(), flip(), and rewind()

Before using a buffer for input or output, we need to make sure the buffer is correctly prepared with *position* and *limit* set to the proper values. Consider a CharBuffer created with capacity seven, which has been populated by successive calls to put() or read():

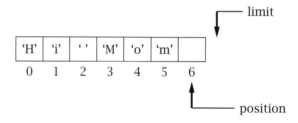

If we now want to use this buffer to do a channel write, since write() will start getting data at *position*, and stop at *limit*, we need to set *limit* to the current value of *position*, and set *position* to 0.

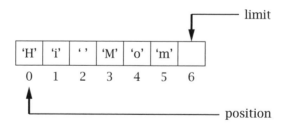

We could handle this ourselves, but fortunately Java provides some convenience methods to do the work for us; they are shown in Table 5.3.

Note that these methods *do not change the buffer's data*, only its indices. The clear() method prepares the buffer to accept new data from a buffer put or channel read by setting *position* to zero and *limit* to *capacity*. Continuing the example above, after clear() the situation looks like this:

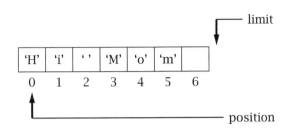

ByteBuffer **Method**	**Prepares Buffer for**	**Resulting Value of**		
		Position	**Limit**	**Mark**
ByteBuffer clear()	read()/put() into buffer	0	*capacity*	undefined
ByteBuffer flip()	write()/get() from buffer	0	*position*	undefined
ByteBuffer rewind()	rewrite()/get() from buffer	0	unchanged	undefined

Table 5.3: Instance Methods of ByteBuffer

Subsequent calls to put()/read() fill the buffer, starting from the first element and filling up to the limit, which is set to the capacity.

```
// Start with buffer in unknown state
buffer.clear();       // Prepare buffer for input, ignoring existing state
channel.read(buffer); // Read new data into buffer, starting at first element
```

Despite its name, clear() doesn't actually change the buffer's data; it simply resets the buffer's main index values. Consider a buffer recently populated with data (say, 3 characters) from put() and/or read(). The *position* value indicates the first element that does not contain valid data:

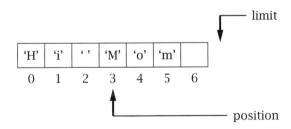

The flip() method prepares for data transfer *out* of the buffer, by setting *limit* to the current position and *position* to zero:

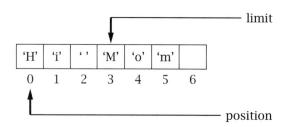

Subsequent calls to get()/write() retrieve data from the buffer starting from the first element and proceeding up to the *limit*. Here is an example of flip()'s usage:

```
// ... put data in buffer with put() or read() ...
buffer.flip();                      // Set position to 0, limit to old position
while (buffer.hasRemaining())  // Write buffer data from the first element up to limit
  channel.write(buffer);
```

Suppose you've written some or all of the data from a buffer and you'd like to go back to the beginning of the buffer to write the same information again (for example, you want to send it on another channel). The rewind() method sets *position* to zero and invalidates the *mark*. It's similar to flip() except *limit* remains unchanged. When might you use this? Well, you might want to write everything you send over the network to a logger:

```
// Start with buffer ready for writing
while (buffer.hasRemaining())      // Write all data to network
  networkChannel.write(buffer);
buffer.rewind();                   // Reset buffer to write again
while (buffer.hasRemaining())      // Write all data to logger
  loggerChannel.write(buffer);
```

5.4.5 Compacting Data in a Buffer

The compact() operation copies the elements between *position* and *limit* to the start of the buffer, to make room for subsequent put()/read() calls. The value of *position* is set to the length of the copied data, the value of *limit* is set to the capacity, and *mark* becomes undefined. Consider the following buffer state before compact() is called:

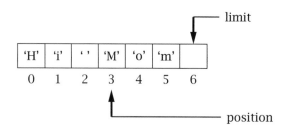

Here is the situation after compact():

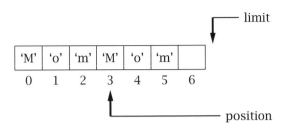

Why use this operation? Suppose you have a buffer for writing data. Recall that a nonblocking call to write() only uses the data it can send without blocking; therefore, write() will not necessarily send all elements of the buffer. Now you need to read() new data into the buffer, after the unwritten data. One way to handle this is to simply set *position = limit* and *limit = capacity*. Of course, you'll need to reset these values later, after reading but before you call write() again. The problem is that eventually the buffer will run out of space; in the figures above, there would only be room for one more byte. Moreover, any space at the beginning of the buffer is wasted. This is exactly the problem compact() is designed to solve. By calling compact() after the write() but before the read() that will add more data, we move all the "left over" data to the start of the buffer, freeing up the maximum space for new data.

```
// Start with buffer ready for reading
while (channel.read(buffer) != -1) {
  buffer.flip();
  channel.write(buffer);
  buffer.compact();
}
while (buffer.hasRemaining())
  channel.write(buffer);
```

Note, however, that as we mentioned at the beginning of the chapter, copying data is a rather expensive operation, so compact() should be used sparingly.

5.4.6 Buffer Perspectives: duplicate(), slice(), etc.

NIO provides several ways of creating a new buffer that shares content with a given buffer, but differs on the processing of the elements. Basically, the new buffer has its own independent state variables (position, limit, capacity, and mark) but shares the backing storage with the original buffer. Any changes to the new buffer are shared with the original. Think of this as an alternate perspective on the same data. Table 5.4 lists the relevant methods.

The duplicate() method creates a new buffer that shares the content of the original buffer. The new buffer's position, limit, mark, and capacity initially match the original buffer's index

Method	New Buffer's Initial Value of			
	Capacity	**Position**	**Limit**	**Mark**
ByteBuffer duplicate()	*capacity*	*position*	*limit*	*mark*
ByteBuffer slice()	remaining()	0	remaining()	undefined
ByteBuffer asReadOnlyBuffer()	*capacity*	*position*	*limit*	*mark*
CharBuffer asCharBuffer()	remaining()/2	0	remaining()/2	undefined
DoubleBuffer asDoubleBuffer()	remaining()/8	0	remaining()/8	undefined
FloatBuffer asFloatBuffer()	remaining()/4	0	remaining()/4	undefined
IntBuffer asIntBuffer()	remaining()/4	0	remaining()/4	undefined
LongBuffer asLongBuffer()	remaining()/8	0	remaining()/8	undefined
ShortBuffer asShortBuffer()	remaining()/2	0	remaining()/2	undefined

Table 5.4: Methods for Creating Different Perspectives on a Buffer

values; however, the values are independent. Since the content is shared, changes to the original buffer or any duplicates will be visible to all. Let's return to our example above where you want to write everything you send over the network to a logger.

```
// Start with buffer ready for writing
ByteBuffer logBuffer = buffer.duplicate();
while (buffer.hasRemaining())      // Write all data to network
  networkChannel.write(buffer);
while (logBuffer.hasRemaining())      // Write all data to logger
  loggerChannel.write(buffer);
```

Note that with buffer duplication, writing to the network and log could be done in parallel using different threads.

The slice() method creates a new buffer that shares some subsequence of the original buffer. The new buffer's position is zero, and its limit and capacity are both equal to the difference between the limit and position of the original buffer. slice() sets the new buffer's array offset to the original buffer's position; however, calling array() on the new buffer still returns the entire array.

Channel reads and writes take only ByteBuffers; however, we may be interested in communicating using other primitive types. A ByteBuffer can create a separate "view buffer" that interprets its contents as some other primitive type (e.g., CharBuffer). Data of the new type can then be read from (and written to, although that is an optional operation) this buffer. The new buffer shares the backing storage of the original ByteBuffer; therefore, changes to either buffer are seen in both new and original buffers. A newly created view buffer has its *position* set to zero, and its contents start at the original buffer's *position*. This is very similar to the slice() operation; however, since the view buffer operates over multibyte elements, the capacity and limit of the new buffer is the remaining number of bytes divided by the number of bytes in the corresponding primitive type (e.g., divide by 8 when creating a DoubleBuffer).

Let's look at an example. Suppose you have received (via some `Channel`) a message that consists of a single byte, followed by a number of two-byte integers (i.e., shorts), in big-endian order. Because the message arrives over a `Channel`, it's in a `ByteBuffer`, buf. The first byte of the message contains the number of two-byte integers that make up the rest of the message. You might call `buf.getShort()` the number of times indicated by the first byte. Or you can get all the integers at once, like this:

```
// ...get message by calling channel.read(buf) ...
int numShorts = (int)buf.get();
if (numShorts < 0) {
    throw new SomeException()
} else {
    short[] shortArray = new short[numShorts];
    ShortBuffer sbuf = buf.asShortBuffer();
    sbuf.get(shortArray);  // note: will throw if header was incorrect!
}
```

The `asReadOnlyBuffer()` method works just like `duplicate()` except that all mutator methods on the new buffer will always throw a ReadOnlyBufferException. This includes all forms of `put()`, `compact()`, etc. Even calls to `array()` and `arrayOffset()` for a nondirect buffer throw this exception. Of course, changes to the non-read-only buffer that generated this read-only buffer will still be shared. Like a buffer created with `duplicate()`, read-only buffers have independent buffer state variables. You can use the `isReadOnly()` method to test if a buffer is read-only. If a buffer is already read-only, calling `duplicate()` or `slice()` will create a read-only buffer.

5.4.7 Character Coding

Recall from Chapter 3 that characters are encoded as sequences of bytes, and that there are various mappings (called charsets) between sets of characters and byte sequences. Another use of NIO buffers is to convert among various charsets. To use this facility, you need to know about two additional classes in the java.nio.charset package (we have already encountered Charset in Chapter 3): CharsetEncoder and CharsetDecoder.

To encode, use a `Charset` instance to create an encoder and call encode:

```
Charset charSet = Charset.forName("US-ASCII");
CharsetEncoder encoder = charSet.newEncoder();
ByteBuffer buffer = encoder.encode(CharBuffer.wrap("Hi mom"));
```

To decode, use the `Charset` instance to create a decoder and call decode:

```
CharsetDecoder decoder = charSet.newDecoder();
CharBuffer cBuf = decoder.decode(buffer);
```

While this approach certainly works, it can be inefficient when coding multiple times. For example, each call to encode/decode creates a new `Byte/CharBuffer`. Other inefficiencies crop up relating to coder creation and operation.

```
encoder.reset();
if (encoder.encode(CharBuffer.wrap("Hi "),buffer,false) == CoderResult.OVERFLOW) {
  // ... deal with lack of space in buffer ...
}
if (encoder.encode(CharBuffer.wrap("Mom"),buffer,true)  == CoderResult.OVERFLOW) {
  // ... ditto ...
}
encoder.flush(buffer);
```

The encode() method converts the given CharBuffer into a byte sequence and writes the bytes to the given buffer. If the buffer is too small, encode() returns a CoderResult.OVERFLOW. If the input is completely consumed and the encoder is ready for more, CoderResult.UNDERFLOW is returned; otherwise the input is malformed in some way, and a CoderResult object is returned that indicates the nature and location of the problem. We set the final boolean parameter to TRUE only when we have reached the end of input to the encoder. flush() pushes any buffered encoder state to the buffer. Note that it is not strictly necessary to call reset(), which sets up the encoder's internal state so it can encode again, on a freshly created encoder.

5.5   Stream (TCP) Channels in Detail

Stream channels come in two varieties: SocketChannel and ServerSocketChannel. Like its Socket counterpart, a SocketChannel is a communication channel for connected endpoints.

SocketChannel: Creating, connecting, and closing

```
static SocketChannel open(SocketAddress remote)
static SocketChannel open()
boolean connect(SocketAddress remote)
boolean isConnected()
void close()
boolean isOpen()
Socket socket()
```

A SocketChannel is created by calling the open() factory method. The first form of open() takes a SocketAddress (see Chapter 2) and returns a SocketChannel connected to the specified server; note that this method may block for an indefinite period. The parameterless form of open() creates an unconnected SocketChannel, which may be connected to an endpoint with the connect() method. When you are finished with a SocketChannel, call the close() method. One important point is that each instance of SocketChannel "wraps" a basic Java Socket, which you may access using the socket() method. This will allow you to call basic Socket methods to bind, set socket options, etc. See TCPEchoClientNonblocking.java (pages 113–114) for an example of SocketChannel creation, connection, and closing.

After you create and connect your SocketChannel, you perform I/O with the channel's read and write methods.

SocketChannel: Reading and writing

```
int read(ByteBuffer dst)
long read(ByteBuffer[] dsts)
long read(ByteBuffer[] dsts, int offset, int length)
int write(ByteBuffer src)
long write(ByteBuffer[] srcs)
long write(ByteBuffer[] srcs, int offset, int length)
```

The most basic form of read takes a single ByteBuffer and reads up to the number of bytes remaining in the buffer. The other form of read takes an array of ByteBuffers and reads up to the number of bytes remaining in all of the buffers by filling each buffer in array order. This is called a *scattering read* because it scatters the incoming bytes over multiple buffers. It's important to note that the scattering read isn't obligated to fill all the buffer(s); the total amount of buffer space is simply an upper bound.

The most basic form of write takes a single ByteBuffer and attempts to write the bytes remaining in the buffer to the channel. The other form of write takes an array of ByteBuffers and attempts to write the bytes remaining in all buffers. This is called a *gathering write* because it gathers up bytes from multiple buffers to send together. See TCPEchoClientNonblocking.java (pages 113–114) and TCPServerSelector.java (pages 116–117) for examples of using read and write.

Like its ServerSocket counterpart, a ServerSocketChannel is a channel for listening for client connections.

ServerSocketChannel: Creating, accepting, and closing

```
static ServerSocketChannel open()
ServerSocket socket()
SocketChannel accept()
void close()
boolean isOpen()
```

A ServerSocketChannel is created by calling the open() factory method. Each instance wraps an instance of ServerSocket, which you can access using the socket() method. As illustrated in the earlier examples, you *must* access the underlying ServerSocket instance to bind it to a desired port, set any socket options, etc. After creating and binding, you are ready to accept client connections by calling the accept() method, which returns the new, connected SocketChannel. When you are finished with a ServerSocketChannel, call the close() method. See TCPServerSelector.java (pages 116–117) for an example of using ServerSocket.

As we've already mentioned, blocking channels provide little advantage over regular sockets, except that they can (must) be used with Buffers. You will therefore almost always be setting your channels to be nonblocking.

SocketChannel, Server SocketChannel: Setting blocking behavior

```
SelectableChannel configureBlocking(boolean block)
boolean isBlocking()
```

To set a SocketChannel or ServerSocketChannel to nonblocking, call configureBlocking(FALSE). The configureBlocking() method returns a SelectableChannel, the superclass of both SocketChannel and ServerSocketChannel.

Consider setting up a connection for a SocketChannel. If you give the open() factory method of SocketChannel a remote address, the call blocks until the connection completes. To avoid this, use the parameterless version of open(), configure the channel to be nonblocking, and call connect(), specifying the remote endpoint address. If the connection can be made without blocking, connect() returns TRUE ; otherwise, you need some way to determine when the socket becomes connected.

SocketChannel: Testing connectivity

```
boolean finishConnect()
boolean isConnected()
boolean isConnectionPending()
```

With a nonblocking SocketChannel, once a connection has been initiated, the underlying socket may be neither connected nor disconnected; instead, a connection is "in progress." Because of the way the underlying protocol mechanisms work (see Chapter 6), the socket may persist in this state for an indefinite time. The finishConnect() method provides a way to check the status of an in-progress connection attempt on a nonblocking socket, or to block until the connection is completed, for a blocking socket. For example, you might configure the channel to be nonblocking, initiate a connection via connect(), do some other work, configure the channel back to blocking, then call finishConnect() to wait until the connection completes. Or you can leave the channel nonblocking and call finishConnect() repeatedly, as in TCPEchoClientNonblocking.java.

The isConnected() method allows you to determine whether the socket is connected so you can avoid having a NotYetConnectedException thrown (say, by read() or write()). You can use isConnectionPending() to check whether a connection has been initiated on this channel. You want to know this because finishConnect() throws NoConnectionPendingException if invoked when one hasn't been.

5.6 Selectors in Detail

The example TCPEchoServerSelector shows the basics of using Selector. Here we consider some of the details.

Selector: Creating and closing

```
static Selector open()
boolean isOpen()
void close()
```

You create a selector by calling the open() factory method. A selector is either "open" or "closed"; it is created open, and stays that way until you tell the system you are finished with it by invoking its close() method. You can tell whether a selector has been closed yet by calling isOpen().

5.6.1 Registering Interest in Channels

As we have seen, each selector has an associated set of channels which it monitors for specific I/O "operations of interest" to that channel. The association between a Selector and a Channel is represented by an instance of SelectionKey. (Note that a Channel instance can register more than one Selector instance, and so can have more than one associated instance of SelectionKey.) The SelectionKey maintains information about the kinds of operations that are of interest for a channel in a *bitmap*, which is just an int in which individual bits have assigned meanings.

The possible operations of interest are defined by constants of the SelectionKey class; each such constant is a *bitmask* (see Section 3.1.3) with exactly one bit set.

SelectionKey: Interest sets

```
static int OP_ACCEPT
static int OP_CONNECT
static int OP_READ
static int OP_WRITE
int interestOps()
SelectionKey interestOps(int ops)
```

We specify an operation set with a bit vector created by OR-ing together the appropriate constants out of OP_ACCEPT, OP_CONNECT, OP_READ, and OP_WRITE. For example, an operation set containing read and write is specified by the expression (OP_READ | OP_WRITE). The interestOps() method with no parameters returns a bitmap in which each bit set indicates an operation for which the channel will be monitored. The other method takes such a bitmap to indicate which operations should be monitored. *Caveat:* Any change to the interest set associated with a key (channel) does not take effect until the associated selector's select() method is next invoked.

SocketChannel, Server SocketChannel: Registering Selectors

```
SelectionKey register(Selector sel, int ops)
SelectionKey register(Selector sel, int ops, Object attachment)
int validOps()
boolean isRegistered()
SelectionKey keyFor(Selector sel)
```

A channel is registered with a selector by calling the channel's register() method. At registration time we specify the initial interest set by means of a bitmap stored in an int (see "SelectionKey: Interest sets" above); register() returns a SelectionKey instance that represents the association between this channel and the given selector. The validOps() method returns a bitmap indicating the set of valid I/O operations for this channel. For a ServerSocketChannel, accept is the only valid operation, while for a SocketChannel, read, write, and connect are valid. For a DatagramChannel() (Section 5.7) only read and write are valid. A channel may only be registered once with a selector, so subsequent calls to register() simply update the operation interest set of the key. You can find out if a channel is registered with any selector by calling the isRegistered() method. The keyFor() method returns the same SelectionKey that was returned when register() was first called, or if the channel is not registered with the given selector.

The following code registers a channel for both reading and writing:

```
SelectionKey key = clientChannel.register(selector,
                    SelectionKey.OP_READ | SelectionKey.OP_WRITE);
```

Figure 5.1 shows a selector with a key set containing keys representing seven registered channels: two server channels on ports 4000 and 4001, and five client channels created from the server channels.

SelectionKey: Retrieving and canceling

```
Selector selector()
SelectableChannel channel()
void cancel()
```

The Selector and Channel instances with which a key is associated are returned by its selector() and channel() methods, respectively. The cancel() method invalidates the key (permanently) and places it in the selector's *canceled set* (Figure 5.1). The key will be removed from all key sets of the selector on the next call to select(), and the associated channel will no longer be monitored (unless it is re-registered).

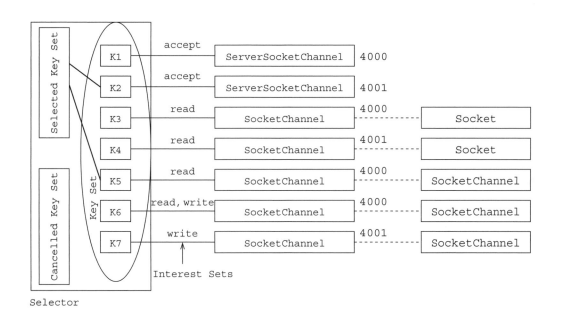

Figure 5.1: Selector with associated key sets.

5.6.2   Selecting and Identifying Ready Channels

With our channels registered with the selector and the associated keys specifying the set of I/O operations of interest, we just need to sit back and wait for I/O. We do this using the selector.

`Selector`: Waiting for channels to be ready ——————————————————————

```
int select()
int select(long timeout)
int selectNow()
Selector wakeup()
```

The select() methods all return a count of how many registered channels are ready for I/O operations in their interest set to be performed. (For example, a channel with OP_READ in the interest set has data ready to be read, or a channel with OP_ACCEPT has a connection ready to accept.) The three methods differ only in their blocking behavior. The parameterless method blocks until at least one registered channel has at least one operation in its interest set ready, or another thread invokes this selector's wakeup() method (in which case it may return 0). The form that takes a timeout parameter blocks until at least one channel is ready, or until the indicated (positive) number of milliseconds has elapsed, or another thread calls wakeup(). The selectNow() is a nonblocking version: it always returns immediately; if no channels are ready, it returns 0. The wakeup() method causes any invocation of one of the select methods that is currently blocked (i.e., in another thread) to return immediately, or, if none is currently blocked, the next invocation of any of the three select methods will return immediately.

After selection, we need to know which channels have ready I/O of interest. Each selector maintains a selected-key set containing the keys from the key set whose associated channels have impending I/O of interest. We access the selected-key set by calling the selectedKeys() method of the selector, which returns a set of SelectionKeys. We can then iterate over this set of keys, handling pending I/O for each:

```
Iterator<SelectionKey> keyIter = selector.selectedKeys().iterator();
while (keyIter.hasNext()) {
  SelectionKey key = keyIter.next();
  // ...Handle I/O for key's channel...
  keyIter.remove();
}
```

The selector in Figure 5.1 has two keys in its selected-key set: K2 and K5.

Selector: Getting key sets

```
Set<SelectionKey> keys()
Set<SelectionKey> selectedKeys()
```

These methods return the selector's different key sets. The keys() method returns *all* currently registered keys. The returned key set is immutable: any attempt to directly modify it (e.g., by calling its remove() method) will result in an UnsupportedOperation-Exception. The selectedKeys() method returns those keys that were "selected" as having ready I/O operations during the last call to select(). *Caveat:* The set returned by selectedKeys() *is* mutable, and in fact *must* be emptied "manually" between calls to select(). In other words, the select methods only *add* keys to the selected key set; they do not create a new set.

The selected-key set tells us which channels have available I/O. For each of these channels, we need to know the specific ready I/O operations. In addition to the interest set, each key also maintains a set of pending I/O operations called its *ready set*.

SelectionKey: Find ready I/O operations

```
int readyOps()
boolean isAcceptable()
boolean isConnectable()
boolean isReadable()
boolean isValid()
boolean isWritable()
```

We can determine which operations in the interest set are available for a given key by using either the readyOps() method or the other predicate methods. readyOps() returns the entire ready set as a bitmap. The other methods allow each operation to be tested individually.

For example, to see if the channel associated with a key has a read pending we can either use:

```
(key.readyOps() & SelectionKey.OP_READ) != 0
```

or

```
key.isReadable()
```

The keys in a selector's selected-key set and the operations in each key's ready set are determined by select(). Over time, this information can become stale. Some other thread may handle the ready I/O. Also, keys don't live forever. A key becomes invalid when its associated channel or selector is closed. A key may be explicitly invalidated by calling its cancel() method. You can test the validity of a key by calling its isValid() method. Invalid keys are added to the cancelled-key set of the selector and removed from its key set at the next invocation of any form of select(), or close(). (Of course, removing a key from the key set means that its associated channel will no longer be monitored.)

5.6.3   Channel Attachments

When a channel is ready for I/O, we often need additional information to process the request. For example, with our Echo protocol, when a client channel is ready to write, we need data. Of course, the data we need to write was collected earlier by reading it from the same channel, but where do we store it until it can be written? Another example is the framing procedure from Chapter 3. If a message arrives a few bytes at a time, we may need to store the parts received so far until we have the complete message. In both cases, we need to associate state information with each channel. Well, we're in luck! SelectionKeys make storing per-channel state easy with attachments.

SelectionKey: Find ready I/O operations

```
Object attach(Object ob)
Object attachment()
```

Each key can have one attachment, which can be any object. An attachment can be associated when the channel's register() method is first called, or added directly to the key later, with the attach() method. A key's attachment can be accessed using the SelectionKey's attachment() method.

5.6.4   Selectors in a Nutshell

To summarize, here are the steps in using a Selector:

   I. Create a selector instance.

  II. Register it with various channels, specifying I/O operations of interest for each channel.

 III. Repeatedly:

    1. Call one of the select methods.

    2. Get the list of selected keys.

    3. For each key in the selected-keys set,

      a. Fetch the channel and (if applicable) attachment from the key

b. Determine which operations are ready and perform them. If an accept operation, set the accepted channel to nonblocking and register it with the selector

c. Modify the key's operation interest set if needed

d. Remove the key from the selected-keys set

If selectors tell you when I/O is ready, do you still need nonblocking I/O? Yes. A channel's key in the selected-keys set doesn't guarantee nonblocking I/O because key set information can become stale after `select()`. In addition, a blocking write blocks until all bytes are written; however, an OP_WRITE in the ready set only indicates that at least one byte can be written. In fact, you cannot register a channel with a selector unless it is in nonblocking mode: the `register()` method of `SelectableChannel` throws an `IllegalBlockingModeException` if invoked when the channel is in blocking mode.

5.7 Datagram (UDP) Channels

Java NIO provides datagram (UDP) channels with the `DatagramChannel` class. As with the other forms of `SelectableChannel` we've seen, a `DatagramChannel` adds selection and nonblocking behavior and `Buffer`-based I/O to the capabilities of a `DatagramSocket`.

`DatagramChannel`: Creating, connecting, and closing

```
static DatagramChannel open()
boolean isOpen()
DatagramSocket socket() void close()
```

A `DatagramChannel` is created by calling the `open()` factory method, which creates an unbound `DatagramChannel`. The `DatagramChannel` is simply a wrapper around a basic `DatagramSocket`. You may directly access the particular `DatagramSocket` instance using the `socket()` method. This will allow you to call basic `DatagramSocket` methods to bind, set socket options, etc. When you are finished with a `DatagramChannel`, call the `close()` method.

Once you create a `DatagramChannel`, sending and receiving is fairly straightforward.

`DatagramChannel`: Sending and receiving

```
int send(ByteBuffer src, SocketAddress target)
SocketAddress receive(ByteBuffer dst)
```

The send() method constructs a datagram containing the data from the given ByteBuffer and transmits it to the SocketAddress specifying the destination. The receive() method prepares to accept a datagram into the specified buffer and return the address of the sender. *Caveat:* If the buffer's remaining space is smaller than the datagram, any excess bytes are silently discarded.

The following code segment creates a DatagramChannel and sends the UTF-16 encoded string "Hello" to a UDP server running on the same host on port 5000.

```
DatagramChannel channel = DatagramChannel.open();
ByteBuffer buffer = ByteBuffer.wrap("Hello".getBytes("UTF-16"));
channel.send(buffer, new InetSocketAddress("localhost", 5000));
```

The following code segment creates a DatagramChannel, binds the underlying socket to port 5000, receives a datagram with a maximum of 20 bytes, and converts the bytes to a string using UTF-16 encoding.

```
DatagramChannel channel = DatagramChannel.open();
channel.socket().bind(new InetSocketAddress(5000));
ByteBuffer buffer = ByteBuffer.allocateDirect(20);
SocketAddress address = channel.receive(buffer);
buffer.flip();
String received = Charset.forName("UTF-16").newDecoder().decode(buffer).toString();
```

In the send() example above, we don't explicitly bind to a local port so a random port is chosen for us when send() is called. The corresponding receive() method returns a SocketAddress, which includes the port.

If we're always going to send to and receive from the same remote endpoint, we can optionally call the connect() method and specify the SocketAddress of a remote endpoint.

DatagramChannel: Connecting DatagramChannels

```
DatagramChannel connect(SocketAddress remote)
DatagramChannel disconnect()
boolean isConnected()
int read(ByteBuffer dst)
long read(ByteBuffer[] dsts)
long read(ByteBuffer[] dsts, int offset, int length)
int write(ByteBuffer src)
long write(ByteBuffer[] srcs)
long write(ByteBuffer[] srcs, int offset, int length)
```

These methods restrict us to only sending to and receiving from the specified address. Why do this? One reason is that after connect(), instead of receive() and send(), we can use read() and write(), which don't need to deal with remote addresses. The read() and write() methods receive and send a single datagram. The scattering read, which takes an array of ByteBuffers, only receives a single datagram, filling in the buffers in order. The gathering write transmits a single datagram created by concatenating the bytes from all of the array buffers. *Caveat:* The largest datagram that can be sent today is 65,507 bytes; attempts to send more will be silently truncated.

Another advantage of connect() is that a connected datagram channel may only receive datagrams from the specified endpoint so we don't have to test for spurious reception. Note that connect() for a DatagramChannel does nothing more than restrict send and receive endpoints; no packets are exchanged as they are for connect() on a SocketChannel, and there is no need to wait or test for the connection to be completed, as there is with a SocketChannel. (See Chapter 6.)

So far, DatagramChannels look a lot like DatagramSockets. The major difference between datagram channels and sockets is the ability of a channel to perform nonblocking I/O operations and use selectors. Selector creation, channel registration, selection, etc., work almost identically to the SocketChannel. One difference is that you cannot register for connect I/O operations, but you wouldn't want to, since a DatagramChannel's connect() never blocks anyway.

┌── **DatagramChannel**: Setting blocking behavior and using selectors ──────┐

```
SelectableChannel configureBlocking(boolean block)
boolean isBlocking()
SelectionKey register(Selector sel, int ops)
SelectionKey register(Selector sel, int ops, Object attachment)
boolean isRegistered()
int validOps()
SelectionKey keyFor(Selector sel)
```

These methods have the same behavior as for SocketChannel and ServerSocketChannel.

Let's rewrite our DatagramSocket UDP echo server from Chapter 4 using DatagramChannel. The server listens on the specified port and simply echoes back any datagram it receives. The main difference is that this server doesn't block on send() and receive().

UDPEchoServerSelector.java

```
0  import java.io.IOException;
1  import java.net.InetSocketAddress;
2  import java.net.SocketAddress;
```

```
3    import java.nio.ByteBuffer;
4    import java.nio.channels.DatagramChannel;
5    import java.nio.channels.SelectionKey;
6    import java.nio.channels.Selector;
7    import java.util.Iterator;
8
9    public class UDPEchoServerSelector {
10
11     private static final int TIMEOUT = 3000; // Wait timeout (milliseconds)
12
13     private static final int ECHOMAX = 255; // Maximum size of echo datagram
14
15     public static void main(String[] args) throws IOException {
16
17       if (args.length != 1) // Test for correct argument list
18         throw new IllegalArgumentException("Parameter(s): <Port>");
19
20       int servPort = Integer.parseInt(args[0]);
21
22       // Create a selector to multiplex client connections.
23       Selector selector = Selector.open();
24
25       DatagramChannel channel = DatagramChannel.open();
26       channel.configureBlocking(false);
27       channel.socket().bind(new InetSocketAddress(servPort));
28       channel.register(selector, SelectionKey.OP_READ, new ClientRecord());
29
30       while (true) { // Run forever, receiving and echoing datagrams
31         // Wait for task or until timeout expires
32         if (selector.select(TIMEOUT) == 0) {
33           System.out.print(".");
34           continue;
35         }
36
37         // Get iterator on set of keys with I/O to process
38         Iterator<SelectionKey> keyIter = selector.selectedKeys().iterator();
39         while (keyIter.hasNext()) {
40           SelectionKey key = keyIter.next(); // Key is bit mask
41
42           // Client socket channel has pending data?
43           if (key.isReadable())
44             handleRead(key);
45
46           // Client socket channel is available for writing and
47           // key is valid (i.e., channel not closed).
```

```
48        if (key.isValid() && key.isWritable())
49          handleWrite(key);
50
51        keyIter.remove();
52      }
53    }
54  }
55
56  public static void handleRead(SelectionKey key) throws IOException {
57    DatagramChannel channel = (DatagramChannel) key.channel();
58    ClientRecord clntRec = (ClientRecord) key.attachment();
59    clntRec.buffer.clear();    // Prepare buffer for receiving
60    clntRec.clientAddress = channel.receive(clntRec.buffer);
61    if (clntRec.clientAddress != null) {  // Did we receive something?
62      // Register write with the selector
63      key.interestOps(SelectionKey.OP_WRITE);
64    }
65  }
66
67  public static void handleWrite(SelectionKey key) throws IOException {
68    DatagramChannel channel = (DatagramChannel) key.channel();
69    ClientRecord clntRec = (ClientRecord) key.attachment();
70    clntRec.buffer.flip(); // Prepare buffer for sending
71    int bytesSent = channel.send(clntRec.buffer, clntRec.clientAddress);
72    if (bytesSent != 0) { // Buffer completely written?
73      // No longer interested in writes
74      key.interestOps(SelectionKey.OP_READ);
75    }
76  }
77
78  static class ClientRecord {
79    public SocketAddress clientAddress;
80    public ByteBuffer buffer = ByteBuffer.allocate(ECHOMAX);
81  }
82 }
```

UDPEchoServerSelector.java

5.8 Exercises

1. Modify `TCPEchoClientNonblocking.java` to use a fixed-length write buffer.
2. Write an echo client that uses `Buffer` and `DatagramChannel`.

chapter **6**

Under the Hood

Some of the subtleties of network programming are difficult to grasp without some understanding of the data structures associated with the socket implementation and certain details of how the underlying protocols work. This is especially true of TCP sockets (i.e., instances of Socket). This chapter describes some of what goes on under the hood when you create and use an instance of Socket or ServerSocket. (The initial discussion and Section 6.5 apply as well to DatagramSocket and MulticastSocket. Also, since each SocketChannel has an underlying Socket (and similarly for the other flavors of channels), the discussion applies to them as well. However, most of this chapter focuses on TCP sockets, that is, Socket and Server-Socket.) Please note that this description covers only the normal sequence of events and glosses over many details. Nevertheless, we believe that even this basic level of understanding is helpful. Readers who want the full story are referred to the TCP specification [15] or to one of the more comprehensive treatises on the subject [5,18].

Figure 6.1 is a simplified view of some of the information associated with a Socket instance. The classes are supported by an underlying implementation that is provided by the JVM and/or the platform on which it is running (i.e., the "socket layer" of the host's OS). Operations on the Java objects are translated into manipulations of this underlying abstraction. In this chapter, "Socket" refers generically to one of the classes in Figure 6.1, while "socket" refers to the underlying abstraction, whether it is provided by an underlying OS or the JVM implementation itself (e.g., in an embedded system). It is important to note that other (possibly non-Java) programs running on the same host may be using the network via the underlying

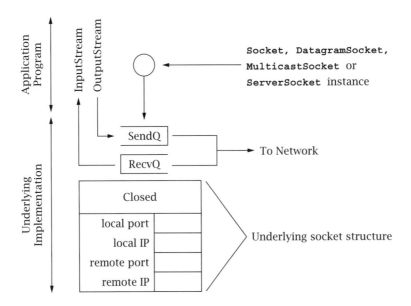

Figure 6.1: Data structures associated with a socket.

socket abstraction, and thus competing with Java Socket instances for resources such as ports.

By "socket structure" here we mean the collection of data structures in the underlying implementation (of both the JVM and TCP/IP, but primarily the latter) that contain the information associated with a particular Socket instance. For example, the socket structure contains, among other information

- The local and remote Internet addresses and port numbers associated with the socket. The local Internet address (labeled "Local IP" in the figure) is one of those assigned to the local host; the local port is set at Socket creation time. The remote address and port identify the remote socket, if any, to which the local socket is connected. We will say more about how and when these values are determined shortly (Section 6.5 contains a concise summary).
- A FIFO queue of received data waiting to be delivered and a queue for data waiting to be transmitted.
- For a TCP socket, additional protocol state information relevant to the opening and closing TCP handshakes. In Figure 6.1, the state is "Closed"; all sockets start out in the Closed state.

Some general-purpose operating systems provide tools that enable users to obtain a "snapshot" of these underlying data structures. One such tool is `netstat`, which is typically available on both Unix (Linux) and Windows platforms. Given appropriate options, `netstat` displays exactly the information indicated in Figure 6.1: number of bytes in *SendQ* and *RecvQ*, local and remote IP addresses and port numbers, and the connection state. Command-line options may vary, but the output should look something like this:

```
Active Internet connections (servers and established)
Proto Recv-Q Send-Q Local Address            Foreign Address        State
tcp        0      0 0.0.0.0:36045            0.0.0.0:*              LISTEN
tcp        0      0 0.0.0.0:111              0.0.0.0:*              LISTEN
tcp        0      0 0.0.0.0:53363            0.0.0.0:*              LISTEN
tcp        0      0 127.0.0.1:25             0.0.0.0:*              LISTEN
tcp        0      0 128.133.190.219:34077    4.71.104.187:80       TIME_WAIT
tcp        0      0 128.133.190.219:43346    79.62.132.8:22        ESTABLISHED
tcp        0      0 128.133.190.219:875      128.133.190.43:2049   ESTABLISHED
tcp6       0      0 :::22                    :::*                  LISTEN
```

The first four lines and the last line depict server sockets listening for connections. (The last line is a listening socket bound to an IPv6 address.) The fifth line corresponds to a connection to a Web server (port 80) that is partially shut down (see Section 6.4.2 below). The next-to-last two lines are existing TCP connections. You may want to play with `netstat`, if it is available on your system, to examine the status of connections in the scenarios depicted below. Be aware, however, that because the transitions between states depicted in the figures happen so quickly, it may be difficult to catch them in the "snapshot" provided by `netstat`.

Knowing that these data structures exist and how they are affected by the underlying protocols is useful because they control various aspects of the behavior of the various Socket objects. For example, because TCP provides a *reliable* byte-stream service, a copy of any data written to a Socket's OutputStream must be kept until it has been successfully received at the other end of the connection. Writing data to the output stream does *not* imply that the data has actually been sent—only that it has been copied into the local buffer. Even flush()ing a Socket's OutputStream doesn't guarantee that anything goes over the wire immediately. Moreover, the nature of the byte-stream service means that message boundaries are *not* preserved in the input stream. As we saw in Section 3.3, this complicates the process of receiving and parsing for some protocols. On the other hand, with a DatagramSocket, packets are *not* buffered for retransmission, and by the time a call to the send() method returns, the data has been given to the network subsystem for transmission. If the network subsystem cannot handle the message for some reason, the packet is silently dropped (but this is rare).

The next three sections deal with some of the subtleties of sending and receiving with TCP's byte-stream service. Then, Section 6.4 considers the connection establishment and termination of the TCP protocol. Finally, Section 6.5 discusses the process of matching incoming packets to sockets and the rules about binding to port numbers.

6.1 Buffering and TCP

As a programmer, the most important thing to remember when using a TCP socket is this:

> **You cannot assume any correspondence between writes to the output stream at one end of the connection and reads from the input stream at the other end.**

In particular, data passed in a single invocation of the output stream's write() method at the sender can be spread across multiple invocations of the input stream's read() method at the other end; and a single read() may return data passed in multiple write()s.

To see this, consider a program that does the following:

```
byte[] buffer0 = new byte[1000];
byte[] buffer1 = new byte[2000];
byte[] buffer2 = new byte[5000];
...
Socket s = new Socket(destAddr, destPort);
OutputStream out = s.getOutputStream();
...
out.write(buffer0);
...
out.write(buffer1);
...
out.write(buffer2);
...
s.close();
```

where the ellipses represent code that sets up the data in the buffers but contains no other calls to out.write(). Throughout this discussion, "in" refers to the InputStream of the receiver's Socket, and "out" refers to the OutputStream of the sender's Socket.

This TCP connection transfers 8000 bytes to the receiver. The way these 8000 bytes are grouped for delivery at the receiving end of the connection depends on the timing between the out.write()s and in.read()s at the two ends of the connection—as well as the size of the buffers provided to the in.read() calls.

We can think of the sequence of all bytes sent (in one direction) on a TCP connection up to a particular instant in time as being divided into three FIFO queues:

1. *SendQ*: Bytes buffered in the underlying implementation at the sender that have been written to the output stream but not yet successfully transmitted to the receiving host.

2. *RecvQ*: Bytes buffered in the underlying implementation at the receiver waiting to be delivered to the receiving program—that is, read from the input stream.

3. *Delivered*: Bytes already read from the input stream by the receiver.

A call to out.write() at the sender appends bytes to *SendQ*. The TCP protocol is responsible for moving bytes—in order—from *SendQ* to *RecvQ*. It is important to realize that this transfer cannot be controlled or directly observed by the user program, and that it occurs in chunks whose sizes are more or less independent of the size of the buffers passed in write()s. Bytes are moved from *RecvQ* to *Delivered* as they are read from the Socket's InputStream by the receiving program; the size of the transferred chunks depends on the amount of data in *RecvQ* and the size of the buffer given to read().

Figure 6.2 shows one possible state of the three queues *after* the three out.write()s in the example above, but *before* any in.read()s at the other end. The different shading patterns denote bytes passed in the three different invocations of write() shown above.

The output of netstat on the sending host at the instant depicted in Figure 6.2 would contain a line like:

```
Active Internet connections
Proto Recv-Q Send-Q Local Address        Foreign Address      State
tcp        0   6500 10.21.44.33:43346     192.0.2.8:22         ESTABLISHED
```

On the receiving host, netstat shows:

```
Active Internet connections
Proto Recv-Q Send-Q Local Address        Foreign Address      State
tcp     1500      0 192.0.2.8:22          10.21.44.33:43346    ESTABLISHED
```

Now suppose the receiver calls read() with a byte array of size 2000. The read() call will move all of the 1500 bytes present in the waiting-for-delivery (*RecvQ*) queue into the byte array and return the value 1500. Note that this data includes bytes passed in both the first and second calls to write(). At some time later, after TCP has completed transfer of more data, the three partitions might be in the state shown in Figure 6.3.

If the receiver now calls read() with a buffer of size 4000, that many bytes will be moved from the waiting-for-delivery (*RecvQ*) queue to the already-delivered (*Delivered*) queue; this includes the remaining 1500 bytes from the second write(), plus the first 2500 bytes from the third write(). The resulting state of the queues is shown in Figure 6.4.

The number of bytes returned by the next call to read() depends on the size of the buffer and the timing of the transfer of data over the network from the send-side socket/TCP

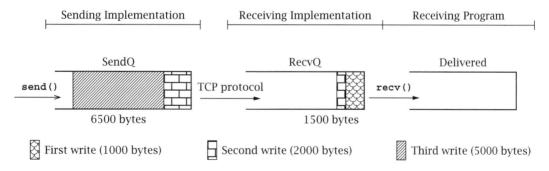

Figure 6.2: State of the three queues after three writes.

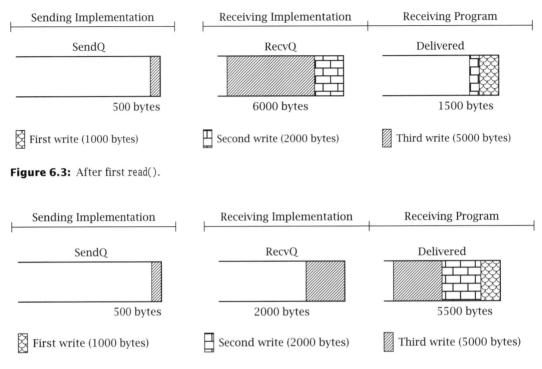

Figure 6.3: After first read().

Figure 6.4: After another read().

implementation to the receive-side implementation. The movement of data from the *SendQ* to the *RecvQ* buffer has important implications for the design of application protocols. We have already encountered the need to parse messages as they are received via a Socket when in-band delimiters are used for framing (see Section 3.3). In the following sections, we consider two more subtle ramifications.

6.2 Deadlock Danger

Application protocols have to be designed with some care to avoid *deadlock*—that is, a state in which each peer is blocked waiting for the other to do something. For example, it is pretty obvious that if both client and server try to receive immediately after a connection is established, deadlock will result. Deadlock can also occur in less immediate ways.

The buffers *SendQ* and *RecvQ* in the implementation have limits on their capacity. Although the actual amount of memory they use may grow and shrink dynamically, a hard limit is necessary to prevent all of the system's memory from being gobbled up by a single TCP connection under control of a misbehaving program. Because these buffers are finite, they can fill up, and it is this fact, coupled with TCP's *flow control* mechanism, that leads to the possibility of another form of deadlock.

Once *RecvQ* is full, the TCP flow control mechanism kicks in and prevents the transfer of any bytes from the sending host's *SendQ,* until space becomes available in *RecvQ* as a result of the receiver calling the input stream's read() method. (The purpose of the flow control mechanism is to ensure that the sender does not transmit more data than the receiving system can handle.) A sending program can continue to write output until *SendQ* is full; however, once *SendQ* is full, a call to out.write() will block until space becomes available, that is, until some bytes are transferred to the receiving socket's *RecvQ.* If *RecvQ* is also full, everything stops until the receiving program calls in.read() and some bytes are transferred to *Delivered.*

Let's assume the sizes of *SendQ* and *RecvQ* are *SQS* and *RQS*, respectively. A write() call with a byte array of size n such that $n > SQS$ will not return until at least $n - SQS$ bytes have been transferred to *RecvQ* at the receiving host. If n exceeds $(SQS + RQS)$, write() cannot return until after the receiving program has read at least $n - (SQS + RQS)$ bytes from the input stream. If the receiving program does not call read(), a large send() may not complete successfully. In particular, if both ends of the connection invoke their respective output streams' write() method simultaneously with buffers greater than $SQS + RQS$, deadlock will result: neither write will ever complete, and both programs will remain blocked forever.

As a concrete example, consider a connection between a program on Host A and a program on Host B. Assume *SQS* and *RQS* are 500 at both A and B. Figure 6.5 shows what happens when both programs try to send 1500 bytes at the same time. The first 500 bytes of data in the program at Host A have been transferred to the other end; another 500 bytes have been copied into *SendQ* at Host A. The remaining 500 bytes cannot be sent—and therefore out.write() will not return—until space frees up in *RecvQ* at Host B. Unfortunately, the same situation holds in the program at Host B. Therefore, neither program's write() call will ever complete.

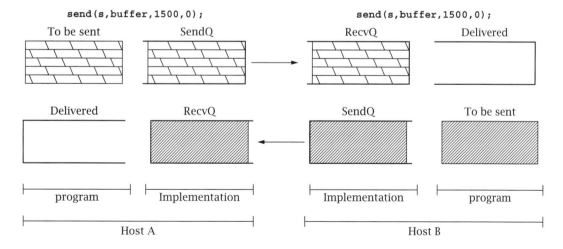

Figure 6.5: Deadlock due to simultaneous write()s to output streams at opposite ends of the connection.

The moral of the story: Design the protocol carefully to avoid sending large quantities of data simultaneously in both directions.

Can this really happen? Let's review the compression protocol example in Section 4.5. Try running the compression client with a large file that is still large *after compression*. The precise definition of "large" here depends on your system, but a file that is already compressed and exceeds 2MB should do nicely. For each read/write, the compression client prints an "R"/"W" to the console. If both the uncompressed and compressed versions of the file are large enough, your client will print a series of Ws and then stop without terminating or printing any Rs.

Why does this happen? The program CompressClient.java sends *all* of the uncompressed data to the compression server *before* it attempts to read anything from the compressed stream. The server, on the other hand, simply reads the uncompressed byte sequence and writes the compressed sequence back to the client. (The number of bytes the server reads before it writes some compressed data depends on the compression algorithm it uses.) Consider the case where *SendQ* and *RecvQ* for both client and server hold 500 bytes each and the client sends a 10,000-byte (uncompressed) file. Suppose also that for this file the server reads about 1000 bytes and then writes 500 bytes, for a 2:1 compression ratio. After the client sends 2000 bytes, the server will eventually have read them all and sent back 1000 bytes, and the client's *RecvQ* and the server's *SendQ* will both be full. After the client sends another 1000 bytes and the server reads them, the server's subsequent attempt to write will block. When the client sends the next 1000 bytes, the client's *SendQ* and the server's *RecvQ* will both fill up. The next client write will block, creating deadlock.

How do we solve this problem? One solution is to execute the client writing and reading loop in separate threads. One thread repeatedly reads uncompressed bytes from a file and sends them to the server until the end of the file is reached, whereupon it calls shutdownOutput() on the socket. The other thread repeatedly reads compressed bytes from the input stream connected to the server and writes them to the output file, until the input stream ends (i.e., the server closes the socket). When one thread blocks, the other thread can proceed independently. We can easily modify our client to follow this approach by putting the call to SendBytes() in CompressClient.java inside a thread as follows:

```
Thread thread = new Thread() {
  public void run() {
    try {
      SendBytes(sock, fileIn);
    } catch (Exception ignored) {}
  }
};
thread.start();
```

See CompressClientNoDeadlock.java on the book's Web site for the complete example.

Of course, the problem can also be solved without using threads, through the use of nonblocking Channels and Selectors, as described in Chapter 5.

6.3   Performance Implications

The TCP implementation's need to copy user data into *SendQ* for potential retransmission also has implications for performance. In particular, the sizes of the *SendQ* and *RecvQ* buffers affect the throughput achievable over a TCP connection. Throughput refers to the rate at which bytes of user data from the sender are made available to the receiving program; in programs that transfer a large amount of data, we want to maximize this rate. In the absence of network capacity or other limitations, bigger buffers generally result in higher throughput.

The reason for this has to do with the cost of transferring data into and out of the buffers in the underlying implementation. If you want to transfer n bytes of data (where n is large), it is generally much more efficient to call write() once with a buffer of size n than it is to call it n times with a single byte.[1] However, if you call write() with a size parameter that is much larger than *SQS* (the size of *SendQ*), the system has to transfer the data from the user address space in *SQS*-sized chunks. That is, the socket implementation fills up the *SendQ* buffer, waits for data to be transferred out of it by the TCP protocol, refills *SendQ*, waits some more, and so on. Each time the socket implementation has to wait for data to be removed from *SendQ*, some time is wasted in the form of overhead (a context switch occurs). This overhead is comparable to that incurred by a completely new call to write(). Thus, the *effective* size of a call to write() is limited by the actual *SQS*. For reading from the InputStream, the same principle applies: however large the buffer we give to read(), it will be copied out in chunks no larger than *RQS*, with overhead incurred between chunks.

If you are writing a program for which throughput is an important performance metric, you will want to change the send and receive buffer sizes using the setSendBufferSize() and setReceiveBufferSize() methods of Socket. Although there is always a system-imposed maximum size for each buffer, it is typically significantly larger than the default on modern systems. Remember that these considerations apply only if your program needs to send an amount of data significantly larger than the buffer size, all at once. Note also that these factors may make little difference if the program deals with some higher-level stream derived from the Socket's basic input stream (say, by using it to create an instance of FilterOutputStream or PrintWriter), which may perform its own internal buffering or add other overhead.

6.4   TCP Socket Life Cycle

When a new instance of the Socket class is created—either via one of the public constructors or by calling the accept() method of a ServerSocket—it can immediately be used for sending and receiving data. That is, when the instance is returned, it is already connected to a

---

[1] The same thing generally applies to reading data from the Socket's InputStream, although calling read() with a larger buffer does not guarantee that more data will be returned.

remote peer and the opening TCP message exchange, or handshake, has been completed by the implementation.

Let us therefore consider in more detail how the underlying structure gets to and from the connected, or "Established," state; as you'll see later (see Section 6.4.2), these details affect the definition of reliability and the ability to create a Socket or ServerSocket bound to a particular port.

6.4.1 Connecting

The relationship between an invocation of the Socket constructor and the protocol events associated with connection establishment at the client are illustrated in Figure 6.6. In this and the remaining figures of this section, the large arrows depict external events that cause the underlying socket structures to change state. Events that occur in the application program—that is, method calls and returns—are shown in the upper part of the figure; events such as message arrivals are shown in the lower part of the figure. Time proceeds left to right in these figures. The client's Internet address is depicted as A.B.C.D, while the server's is W.X.Y.Z; the server's port number is Q. (We have depicted IPv4 addresses, but everything here applies to both IPv4 and IPv6.)

When the client calls the Socket constructor with the server's Internet address, W.X.Y.Z, and port, Q, the underlying implementation creates a socket instance; it is initially in the Closed state. If the client did not specify the local address/port in the constructor call, a local port number (P), not already in use by another TCP socket, is chosen by the implementation. The local Internet address is also assigned; if not explicitly specified, the address of the network interface through which packets will be sent to the server is used. The implementation copies the local and remote addresses and ports into the underlying socket structure, and initiates the TCP connection establishment handshake.

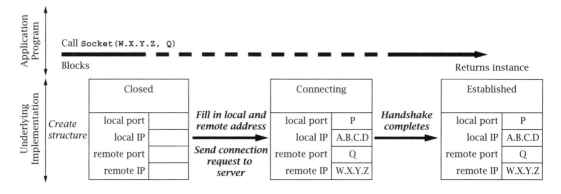

Figure 6.6: Client-side connection establishment.

The TCP opening handshake is known as a *3-way handshake* because it typically involves three messages: a connection request from client to server, an acknowledgment from server to client, and another acknowledgment from client back to server. The client TCP considers the connection to be established as soon as it receives the acknowledgment from the server. In the normal case, this happens quickly. However, the Internet is a best-effort network, and either the client's initial message or the server's response can get lost. For this reason, the TCP implementation retransmits handshake messages multiple times, at increasing intervals. If the client TCP does not receive a response from the server after some time, it *times out* and gives up. In this case the constructor throws an IOException. The connection timeout is generally long, and thus it can take on the order of minutes for a Socket constructor to fail.

After the initial handshake message is sent and before the reply from the server is received (i.e., the middle part of Figure 6.6), the output from netstat on the client host would look something like:

```
Active Internet connections
Proto Recv-Q Send-Q Local Address   Foreign Address      State
tcp        0      0 A.B.C.D:P        W.X.Y.Z:Q            SYN_SENT
```

where "SYN_SENT" is the technical name of the client's state between the first and second messages of the handshake.

If the server is not accepting connections—say, if there is no program associated with the given port at the destination—the server-side TCP will send a rejection message instead of an acknowledgment, and the constructor will throw an IOException almost immediately. Otherwise, after the client receives a positive reply from the server, the netstat output would look like:

```
Active Internet connections
Proto Recv-Q Send-Q Local Address   Foreign Address      State
tcp        0      0 A.B.C.D:P        W.X.Y.Z:Q            ESTABLISHED
```

The sequence of events at the server side is rather different; we describe it in Figures 6.7, 6.8, and 6.9. The server first creates an instance of ServerSocket associated with its well-known port (here, Q). The socket implementation creates an underlying socket structure for the new ServerSocket instance, and fills in Q as the local port and the special *wildcard address* ("*" in the figures) for the local IP address. (The server may also specify a local IP address in the constructor, but typically it does not. In case the server host has more than one IP address, not specifying the local address allows the socket to receive connections addressed to any of the server host's addresses.) The state of the socket is set to "LISTENING", indicating that it is ready to accept incoming connection requests addressed to its port. This sequence is depicted in Figure 6.7. The output from netstat on the server would include a line like:

```
Active Internet connections
Proto Recv-Q Send-Q Local Address   Foreign Address      State
tcp        0      0 0.0.0.0:Q        0.0.0.0:0            LISTENING
```

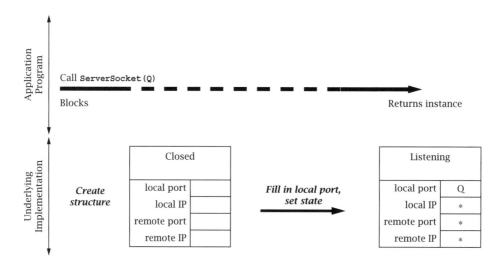

Figure 6.7: Server-side socket setup.

The server can now call the ServerSocket's accept() method, which blocks until the TCP opening handshake has been completed with some client and a new connection has been established. We therefore focus (in Figure 6.8) on the events that occur in the TCP implementation when a client connection request arrives. Note that everything depicted in this figure happens "under the covers," in the TCP implementation.

When the request for a connection arrives from the client, a new socket structure is created for the connection. The new socket's addresses are filled in based on the arriving packet: the packet's destination Internet address and port (W.X.Y.Z and Q, respectively) become the local Internet address and port; the packet's source address and port (A.B.C.D and P) become the remote Internet address and port. Note that the local port number of the new socket is always the same as that of the ServerSocket. The new socket's state is set to indicate that it is "Connecting" (technically called SYN_RCVD at the server side), and it is added to a list of not-quite-connected sockets associated with the socket structure of the ServerSocket. Note that the ServerSocket itself does not change state, nor does any of its address information change. At this point the output of netstat should show both the original, listening socket and the newly created one:

```
Active Internet connections
Proto Recv-Q Send-Q Local Address      Foreign Address      State
tcp      0      0 0.0.0.0:Q            0.0.0.0:0            LISTENING
tcp      0      0 W.X.Y.Z:Q           A.B.C.D:P            SYN_RCVD
```

In addition to creating a new underlying socket structure, the server-side TCP implementation sends an acknowledging TCP handshake message back to the client. However, the server

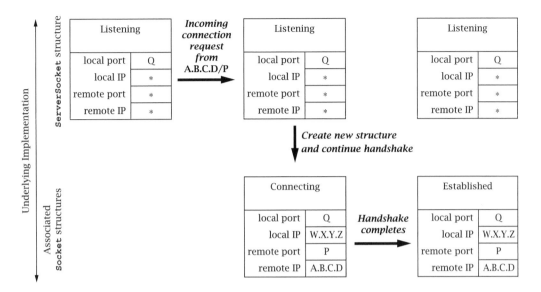

Figure 6.8: Incoming connection request processing.

TCP does not consider the handshake complete until the third message of the 3-way handshake is received from the client. When that message eventually arrives, the new structure's state is set to "ESTABLISHED", and it is then (and only then) moved to a list of socket structures associated with the ServerSocket structure, which represent established connections ready to be accept()ed via the ServerSocket. (If the third handshake message fails to arrive, eventually the "Connecting" structure is deleted.) Output from netstat would include:

```
Active Internet connections
Proto Recv-Q Send-Q Local Address   Foreign Address   State
tcp     0       0 0.0.0.0:Q         0.0.0.0:0         LISTENING
tcp     0       0 W.X.Y.Z:Q         A.B.C.D:P         ESTABLISHED
```

Now we can consider (in Figure 6.9) what happens when the server program calls the ServerSocket's accept() method. The call unblocks as soon as there is something in its associated list of socket structures for new connections. (Note that this list may already be non-empty when accept() is called.) At that time, one of the new connection structures is removed from the list, and an instance of Socket is created for it and returned as the result of the accept().

It is important to note that each structure in the ServerSocket's associated list represents a fully established TCP connection with a client at the other end. Indeed, the client can send data as soon as it receives the second message of the opening handshake—which may be long before the server calls accept() to get a Socket instance for it.

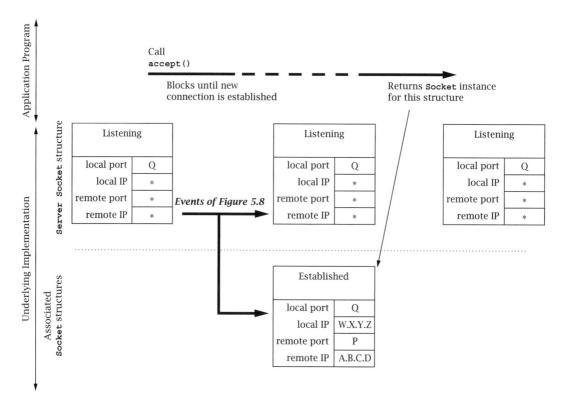

Figure 6.9: accept() processing.

6.4.2   Closing a TCP Connection

TCP has a *graceful close* mechanism that allows applications to terminate a connection without having to worry about loss of data that might still be in transit. The mechanism is also designed to allow data transfers in each direction to be terminated independently, as in the compression example of Section 4.5. It works like this: the application indicates that it is finished sending data on a connected socket by calling close() or by calling shutdownOutput(). At that point, the underlying TCP implementation first transmits any data remaining in *SendQ* (subject to available space in *RecvQ* at the other end), and then sends a closing TCP handshake message to the other end. This closing handshake message can be thought of as an end-of-stream marker: it tells the receiving TCP that no more bytes will be placed in *RecvQ*. (Note that the closing handshake message itself is *not* passed to the receiving application, but that its position in the byte stream is indicated by read() returning −1.) The closing TCP waits for an acknowledgment of its closing handshake message, which indicates that all data sent on the connection made it safely to *RecvQ*. Once that acknowledgment is received, the connection is "Half closed." The connection is not *completely* closed until a symmetric handshake happens in the other direction—that is, until *both* ends have indicated that they have no more data to send.

The closing event sequence in TCP can happen in two ways: either one application calls close() (or shutdownOutput()) and completes its closing handshake before the other calls close(), or both call close() simultaneously, so that their closing handshake messages cross in the network. Figure 6.10 shows the sequence of events in the implementation when the application on one end invokes close() *before* the other end closes. The closing handshake message is sent, the state of the socket structure is set to indicate that it is "Closing," (technically called "FIN_WAIT_1") and the call returns. After this point, further reads and writes on the Socket are disallowed (they throw an exception). When the acknowledgment for the close handshake is received, the state changes to "Half closed" (technically, "FIN_WAIT_2") where it remains until the other end's close handshake message is received. At this point the output of netstat on the client would show the status of the connection as:

```
Active Internet connections
Proto Recv-Q Send-Q Local Address    Foreign Address    State
tcp       0      0 A.B.C.D:P         W.X.Y.Z:Q          FIN_WAIT_2
```

(FIN_WAIT_2 is the technical name for the "Half-closed" state at the host that initiates close first. The state denoted by "Closing" in the figure is technically called FIN_WAIT_1, but it is transient and is difficult to catch with netstat.)

Note that if the remote endpoint goes away while the connection is in this state, the local underlying structure will stay around indefinitely. When the other end's close handshake message arrives, an acknowledgment is sent and the state is changed to "Time-Wait." Although the corresponding Socket instance in the application program may have long since vanished, the associated underlying structure continues to exist in the implementation for a minute or more; the reasons for this are discussed on page 163.

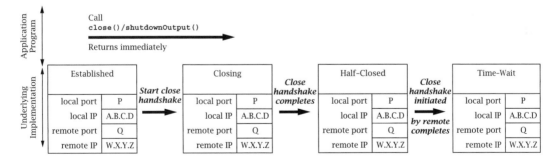

Figure 6.10: Closing a TCP connection first.

The output of `netstat` at the right end of Figure 6.10 includes:

```
Active Internet connections
Proto Recv-Q Send-Q Local Address    Foreign Address    State
tcp      0      0 A.B.C.D:P           W.X.Y.Z:Q          TIME_WAIT
```

Figure 6.11 shows the simpler sequence of events at the endpoint that does not close first. When the closing handshake message arrives, an acknowledgment is sent immediately, and the connection state becomes "Close-Wait." The output of `netstat` on this host shows:

```
Active Internet connections
Proto Recv-Q Send-Q Local Address    Foreign Address    State
tcp      0      0 W.X.Y.Z:Q           A.B.C.D:P          CLOSE_WAIT
```

At this point, we are just waiting for the application to invoke the Socket's close() method. When it does, the final close handshake is initiated and the underlying socket structure is deallocated, although references to its original Socket instance may persist in the Java program.

In view of the fact that both close() and shutdownOutput() return without waiting for the closing handshake to complete, you may wonder how the sender can be assured that sent data has actually made it to the receiving program (i.e., to *Delivered*). In fact, it is possible for an application to call close() or shutdownOutput() and have it complete successfully (i.e., not throw an Exception) *while there is still data in SendQ.* If either end of the connection then crashes before the data makes it to *RecvQ*, data may be lost without the sending application knowing about it.

The best solution is to design the application protocol so that the side that calls close() first does so *only after* receiving application-level assurance that its data was received. For example, when our TCPEchoClient program receives the echoed copy of the data it sent, it knows there is nothing more in transit in either direction, so it is safe to close the connection.

Java does provide a way to modify the behavior of the Socket's close() method, namely, the setSoLinger() method. setSoLinger() controls whether close() waits for the closing

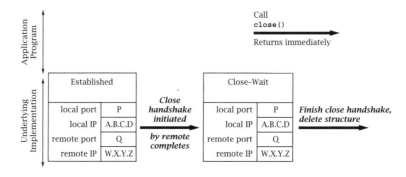

Figure 6.11: Closing after the other end closes.

handshake to complete before returning. It takes two parameters, a boolean that indicates whether to wait, and an integer specifying the number of seconds to wait before giving up. That is, when a timeout is specified via setSoLinger(), close() blocks until the closing hand-shake is completed, or until the specified amount of time passes. At the time of this writing, however, close() provides no indication that the closing handshake failed to complete, even if the time limit set by setSoLinger() expires before the closing sequence completes. In other words, setSoLinger() does not provide any additional assurance to the application in current implementations.

The final subtlety of closing a TCP connection revolves around the need for the Time-Wait state. The TCP specification requires that when a connection terminates, at least one of the sockets persists in the Time-Wait state for a period of time after both closing handshakes complete. This requirement is motivated by the possibility of messages being delayed in the network. If both ends' underlying structures go away as soon as both closing handshakes complete, and a *new* connection is immediately established between the same pair of socket addresses, a message from the previous connection, which happened to be delayed in the network, could arrive just after the new connection is established. Because it would contain the same source and destination addresses, the old message could be mistaken for a message belonging to the new connection, and its data might (incorrectly) be delivered to the application.

Unlikely though this scenario may be, TCP employs multiple mechanisms to prevent it, including the Time-Wait state. The Time-Wait state ensures that every TCP connection ends with a quiet time, during which no data is sent. The quiet time is supposed to be equal to twice the maximum amount of time a packet can remain in the network. Thus, by the time a connection goes away completely (i.e., the socket structure leaves the Time-Wait state and is deallocated) and clears the way for a new connection between the same pair of addresses, no messages from the old instance can still be in the network. In practice, the length of the quiet time is implementation dependent, because there is no real mechanism that limits how long a packet can be delayed by the network. Values in use range from 4 minutes down to 30 seconds or even shorter.

The most important consequence of Time-Wait is that as long as the underlying socket structure exists, no other socket is permitted to be associated with the same local port. In particular, any attempt to create a Socket instance using that port will throw an IOException.

6.5 Demultiplexing Demystified

The fact that different sockets on the same machine can have the same local address and port number is implicit in the discussions above. For example, on a machine with only one IP address, every new Socket instance accept()ed via a ServerSocket will have the same local port number as the ServerSocket. Clearly the process of deciding to which socket an incoming packet should be delivered—that is, the *demultiplexing* process—involves looking at more than just the packet's destination address and port. Otherwise there could be ambiguity about which

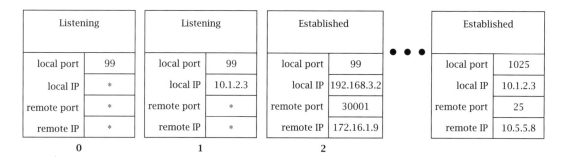

Figure 6.12: Demultiplexing with multiple matching sockets.

socket an incoming packet is intended for. The process of matching an incoming packet to a socket is actually the same for both TCP and UDP, and can be summarized by the following points:

- The local port in the socket structure *must* match the destination port number in the incoming packet.
- Any address fields in the socket structure that contain the wildcard value (*) are considered to match *any* value in the corresponding field in the packet.
- If there is more than one socket structure that matches an incoming packet for all four address fields, the one that matches using the fewest wildcards gets the packet.

For example, consider a host with two IP addresses, 10.1.2.3 and 192.168.3.2, and with a subset of its active TCP socket structures shown in Figure 6.12. The structure labeled 0 is associated with a ServerSocket and has port 99 with a wildcard local address. Socket structure 1 is also for a ServerSocket on the same port, but with the local IP address 10.1.2.3 specified (so it will only accept connection requests to that address). Structure 2 is for a connection that was accepted via the ServerSocket for structure 0, and thus has the same local port number, but also has its local and remote Internet addresses filled in. Other sockets belong to other active connections. Now consider a packet with source IP address 172.16.1.10, source port 56789, destination IP address 10.1.2.3, and destination port 99. It will be delivered to the socket associated with structure 1, because that one matches with the fewest wildcards.

When a program attempts to create a socket with a particular local port number, the existing sockets are checked to make sure that no socket is already using that local port. A Socket constructor will throw an exception if *any* socket matches the local port and local IP address (if any) specified in the constructor. This can cause problems in the following scenario:

1. A client program creates a Socket with a specific local port number, say, *P*, and uses it to communicate with a server.

2. The client closes the Socket, and the underlying structure goes into the Time-Wait state.

3. The client program terminates and is immediately restarted.

If the new incarnation of the client attempts to use the same local port number, the Socket constructor will throw an IOException, because of the other structure in the Time-Wait state. As of this writing, the only way around this is to wait until the underlying structure leaves the Time-Wait state.

So what determines the local/foreign address/port? For a ServerSocket, all constructors require the local port. The local address may be specified to the constructor; otherwise, the local address is the wildcard (*) address. The foreign address and port for a ServerSocket are always wildcards. For a Socket, all constructors require specification of the foreign address and port. The local address and/or port may be specified to the constructor. Otherwise, the local address is the address of the network interface through which the connection to the server is established, and the local port is a randomly selected, unused port number greater than 1023. For a Socket instance returned by accept(), the local address is the destination address from the initial handshake message from the client, the local port is the local port of the ServerSocket, and the foreign address/port is the local address/port of the client. For a DatagramSocket, the local address and/or port may be specified to the constructor. Otherwise the local address is the wildcard address, and the local port is a randomly selected, unused port number greater than 1023. The foreign address and port are initially both wildcards, and remain that way unless the connect() method is invoked to specify particular values.

6.6 Exercises

1. The TCP protocol is designed so that simultaneous connection attempts will succeed. That is, if an application using port P and Internet address W.X.Y.Z attempts to connect to address A.B.C.D, port Q, at the same time as an application using the same address and port tries to connect to W.X.Y.Z, port P, they will end up connected to each other. Can this be made to happen when the programs use the sockets API?

2. The first example of "buffer deadlock" in this chapter involves the programs on both ends of a connection trying to send large messages. However, this is not necessary for deadlock. How could the TCPEchoClient from Chapter 2 be made to deadlock when it connects to the TCPEchoServer from that chapter?

Bibliography

[1] Arnold, Ken, Gosling, James, and Holmes, David, *The Java Programming Language, Fourth Edition*, Addison Wesley, 2006.

[2] Braden, R., editor, "Requirements for Internet Hosts—Communication Layers," Internet Request for Comments 1122, October 1989.

[3] Braden, R., editor, "Requirements for Internet Hosts—Applications and Support," Internet Request for Comments 1123, October 1989.

[4] Comer, Douglas E., *Internetworking with TCP/IP, Volume I: Principles, Protocols, and Architecture* (fourth edition), Prentice-Hall, 2000.

[5] Comer, Douglas E., and Stevens, David L., *Internetworking with TCP/IP, Volume II: Design, Implementation, and Internals* (third edition), Prentice-Hall, 1999.

[6] Comer, Douglas E., and Stevens, David L., *Internetworking with TCP/IP, Volume III: Client-Server Programming and Applications* (Linux/POSIX Sockets Version), Prentice-Hall, 2001.

[7] Deering, S., and Hinden, R, "Internet Protocol, Version 6 (IPv6) Specification," Internet Request for Comments 2460, December 1998.

[8] Freed, Ned, and Postel, J., "IANA Charset Registration Procedures," Internet Request for Comments 2278, January 1998.

[9] Goetz, Brian, with T. Peierls, J. Bloch, J. Bowbeer, D. Holmes, and D. Lea, *Java Concurrency in Practice*, Pearson Education, 2006.

[10] Mockapetris, Paul, "Domain Names—Concepts and Facilities," Internet Request for Comments 1034, November 1987.

[11] Mockapetris, Paul, "Domain Names—Implementation and Specification," Internet Request for Comments 1035, November 1987.

[12] Peterson, Larry L., and Davie, Bruce S., *Computer Networks: A Systems Approach* (third edition), Morgan Kaufmann, 2003.

[13] Postel, John, "User Datagram Protocol," Internet Request for Comments 768, August 1980.

[14] Postel, John, "Internet Protocol," Internet Request for Comments 791, September 1981.

[15] Postel, John, "Transmission Control Protocol," Internet Request for Comments 793, September 1981.

[16] Stevens, W. Richard, *UNIX Network Programming: Networking APIs: Sockets and XTI* (second edition), Prentice-Hall, 1997.

[17] Stevens, W. Richard, *TCP/IP Illustrated, Volume 1: The Protocols*, Addison-Wesley, 1994.

[18] Wright, Gary R., and Stevens, W. Richard, *TCP/IP Illustrated, Volume 2: The Implementation*, Addison Wesley, 1995.

[19] The Unicode Consortium, *The Unicode Standard, Version 5.0*, Addison Wesley, 2006.

Index